BRINGING UP BABY
Three Steps to Making Good
Decisions in Your Child's First Years

BRINGING UP BABY
Three Steps to Making Good Decisions in Your Child's First Years

BY CLAIRE LERNER AND
AMY LAURA DOMBRO

ZERO TO THREE
Washington, D.C.

Published by

ZERO TO THREE
2000 M St., NW, Suite 200
Washington, DC 20036-3307
(202) 638-1144
Toll-free orders (800) 899-4301
Fax: (202) 638-0851
Web: http://www.zerotothree.org

The mission of the ZERO TO THREE Press is to publish authoritative research, practical resources, and new ideas for those who work with and care about infants, toddlers, and their families. Books are selected for publication by an independent Editorial Board. The views contained in this book are those of the authors and do not necessarily reflect those of ZERO TO THREE: National Center for Infants, Toddlers and Families, Inc.

Cover design: Kirk DouPonce, UDG Designworks
Text design and composition: Design Consultants

Library of Congress Cataloging-in-Publication Data

Lerner, Claire.
    Bringing up baby: three steps to making good desisions in your child's first years/Claire Lerner and Amy Laura Dombro. -- 1st ed.
        p. cm.
    Includes bibliographical references.
    ISBN 0-943657-78-4
  1. Child rearing. 2. Parenting. 3. Infants--Care. 4. Infants--Development. 5. Child development. I. Dombro, Amy Laura, 1953- II. Title.
    HQ769.L384 2004
    649'.1--dc22

2004014634

10 9 8 7 6 5 4 3 2 1
ISBN 0-943657-78-4
Printed in the United States of America

Suggested citation:
Lerner, C., & Dombro, A. L. (2005). *Bringing up baby: Three steps to making good decisions in your child's first three years.* Washington, DC: ZERO TO THREE Press.

Acknowledgments

ONE OF THE HUGE BENEFITS OF WORKING WITH ZERO TO THREE is the collaboration and support that are part of every project. This book is no exception. We want to thank our colleagues Rebecca Parlakian, Tom Salyers, and Lynette Kimes for their invaluable feedback from start to finish; Jeree Pawl for her unparalleled wisdom and compassion for the very youngest and those who care for them; and Ross Thompson and Lynne Sturm for making sure we accurately reflected the science of early childhood. We also want to thank Judith Nolte, editor-in-chief of *American Baby*, and Robie Harris for their thoughtful review. To Lynette Ciervo, Roberta Sims, Margaret Cohen, and the many other parents who so openly and generously shared their stories with us, we extend heartfelt appreciation. We could not have written this book without them. Finally, we thank Emily Fenichel, our editor extraordinaire. We are grateful for her sense of humor, sheer brilliance with words, and encouragement and guidance in pushing us to fine-tune and stay true to our message.

A personal note from Claire: I would like to thank my children, Jessica and Sam. You are my inspiration and have given me a deep appreciation of the joy and complexity of raising children. (It should be noted that Jessica also offered invaluable editorial feedback at the ripe age of 10.) Thanks to my mother, Renee, and my brother and sister-in-law, Alan Lerner and Lynnette Santin Lerner (themselves in the thick of raising an adorable toddler), for their meticulous review and keen insights. And thanks to David, for adding levity to this process and for indulging my need to question and discuss every decision that *I* make.

A personal note from Amy: I would like to thank my dad, Bob, for his comment after reading our first draft: "It's a little preachy. Remember, there are many different ways to respond to the same situation." As usual, Dad, you found your way straight to the heart of the matter.

Table of Contents

FOREWORD

OVER THE YEARS, I'VE DISPENSED A FAIR AMOUNT OF CHILD-RAISING advice as the editor of *American Baby* magazine. It's relatively easy to offer answers to the questions most parents have about basic baby care and development, health, and nutrition. These subjects are pretty cut and dried. Once a mom has given a bath, changed a diaper, and fixed a scratched knee, there's not much more you can tell her about how to do it. She quickly becomes an expert at these tasks. But when it comes to explaining her child's behavior and telling her how to handle the sticky situations that come up every day with a young child, then it's not so easy. I've never been able to offer a "one-size-fits-all" solution to these kinds of issues. In fact, there are no simple solutions to understanding the mysteries of a child's mind and why children act the way they do. You can only suggest certain approaches to figuring out the answers.

That's what I like about this new book by the experts at ZERO TO THREE. The authors, Claire Lerner and Amy Dombro, suggest a simple three-step approach that you can use in everyday situations to help you make the best child-rearing decisions. Step 1 is to become self-aware; step 2 is to tune into your child; and step 3 is to then make responsive and sound decisions. Basically, this is like the old axiom, "Know thyself." And then, "Know your child." The book is full of suggestions on how to follow their approach, using tools such as charts and worksheets and then finding myriad examples from parents. With these insights, you'll be armed with enough knowledge to make the best decision about what action to follow in any situation. Take the issue of discipline, for example. Self-awareness means thinking about how you react to your child's behavior—knowing what pushes your buttons. Tuning in to your child means figuring out what a behavior means for him. Is he having a meltdown in the supermarket because he's tired? Or there's too much going on around him? Making responsive decisions means managing your own emotional reaction to his behavior. Once you know what's causing the behavior, you can respond in the most effective way—for example, taking him away from the scene of the tantrum.

I particularly like the authors' advice to look at yourself and analyze your attitudes about parenting and your own behavior. Do you drag yourself to the playground even when you're exhausted, for example, and then find you're so impatient that your child is miserable and you feel like a lousy parent? If you can acknowledge these feelings up front, you're likely to come up with a different plan for the day that can satisfy your child's need for play and yours for, well, just getting through the afternoon. Understanding your own childhood is also a good place to go for discovering where your parenting views came from. What you learned as a child and how you were treated tells you a lot about where your parenting attitudes and values come from.

Temperament—both yours and your child's—is another issue that plays a big role in parenting. It's important to have a good match with your child, but that's not always the case. You might be easygoing but you have a child who reacts intensely to almost every event of the day. To parent effectively, you'll have to learn to respect and accept these differences between you, and separate your needs from your child's. And try to help your child adapt more easily to life's daily demands.

It's also important to recognize that every child is different, and that there's no such thing as a "cookie-cutter" toddler or a single answer to the dilemmas of parenting. A strategy that will help one child calm down after a tantrum might not work for another. It depends, as the authors have made so clear, on the attitude of the parents and the feelings of the child.

Bringing Up Baby will also give you two things that parents need most: reassurance and empowerment. As you use the authors' practical, workable, and encouraging three-step plan, you will experience the power of your parenting. And the joy. If you're going to play in this ballpark, with young kids who are just learning the game, you need the skills and equipment to be on the winning team. And—not to take the sports metaphor too far—hit an occasional home run!

Judith Nolte
Editor in Chief, *American Baby*

A Three-Step Approach to Sensitive and Effective Decision Making

WE HAVE HAD THE GOOD FORTUNE TO TALK AND WORK with hundreds of parents of babies and toddlers over the past 20 years. Between the two of us, we have directed a child-care center for infants and toddlers, worked as a child development specialist in a pediatrician's office, run parenting groups, written parent education materials, and tried as best we could to answer the questions parents have asked us on radio call-in shows and in magazine columns.

As we reflect on thousands of hours of listening to parents, one thing that stands out is their wish for help with the hundreds of parenting decisions they have to make in the first 3 years of their children's lives: Breast or bottle? Sleep with us or in a separate room? Comfort a 6-month-old immediately or let the baby cry it out? Use "time-out" or redirection for a toddler? Allow 1 or 2 hours of TV a day or none? The list is endless.

All of these questions are important. But without knowing you, your child, and the world you share, it is hard to offer relevant and meaningful guidance. What kind of sleep advice could we give that would make sense to parents who want to co-sleep with their child and to parents who want to teach their child to sleep in his own crib? What parenting strategies would work not only for feisty, intense toddlers who hate change but also for flexible, go-with-the-flow kids? What works for one child and one set of parents may not work for another. A one-size-fits-all approach to parenting simply doesn't exist.

In addition, no other parent and child are exactly like you and your child. Each parent and child lives in a unique world of family, friends, community, and culture. Each parent has her own beliefs and values about how to raise a child. All of these factors shape who you are as a parent. One parent may want his child to learn to function well as part of a group; another may place a high value on independence. One parent may value obedience; another may want her child to be a free thinker and to challenge authority.

So we have not written a "how-to" book that offers tips for helping your child stop crying, go to sleep, or use the potty. Instead, we offer a three-step approach to daily decision making for parents and other caregivers of babies and toddlers:

1 Step 1: Develop self-awareness. Think about and understand your own feelings and reactions as a parent—what you bring to your relationship and the situation at hand.

2 Step 2: Tune in to your child. Carefully read your child's cues to understand what she is feeling and thinking as well as what her behavior means.

3 Step 3: Make sensitive and effective decisions. Use what you know about yourself and your child to respond appropriately and to create a path to healthy development.

In the following pages, you will find information about development in the first 3 years, stories from a wide range of parents of babies and toddlers (most are accounts of real children and parents with identifying details disguised; some are composites of many stories we have heard), and tools that will help you use the three-step approach to sensitive and effective decision making. This approach is designed to support you in the process of becoming your own best resource for promoting your child's healthy development in the first 3 years and beyond.

BRINGING UP BABY
Three Steps to Making Good Decisions in Your Child's First Years

CHAPTER ONE
Step 1: Develop Self-Awareness

I couldn't stand it when Sasha (15 months) would cling to me at playgroup while all the other kids were playing and having fun, so I would just leave early. Now I am trying to help Sasha feel more comfortable there by arriving early to let her check out the place and letting her bring her lovey from home. She's slowly getting involved in more of the activities and clings to me a lot less frequently.

When Rubin (26 months) is having a knock-down-drag-out tantrum, and when I manage to stay calm and comfort him (rather than have a tantrum myself!), he pulls it together much more quickly. I've noticed that since I've been doing this, Rubin's tantrums are shorter and fewer.

THE THINGS YOU SAY AND DO—the decisions you make every day as you dress your child, eat breakfast together, play, and set limits—help determine how he develops and who he becomes. You have the power to help your child feel safe and secure and to see himself as smart, confident, and competent. You can help your child learn to cope with strong feelings and reactions and to gain self-control. You can help him learn how to make friends. You can show him the joy of close, positive relationships that lay the foundation for future healthy relationships. The list goes on. Because of the vital role that you play in shaping your child's development, this chapter focuses on helping you become aware of what you do as a parent and why—step 1 in the decision-making process.

Why Think About Yourself?

Parenting is an adventure filled with moments of intense awe, surprise, delight, and challenge. Living with a young child means living in the moment (usually, without enough sleep!). Your hungry baby who is screaming, your toddler who is determined to take every cereal box off the grocery store shelves, and your 3-year-old who yells for you to come right away to watch the new dance he made up all call on you to respond immediately.

Babies and toddlers change so quickly: A newborn who slept for 3-hour stretches one day won't sleep for more than 10 minutes at a time the next. The 9-month-old who last week loved mashed carrots now won't go near a vegetable. The frustrated toddler, who yesterday threw the shoes she couldn't get on by herself, today appears before you, with shoes on and an ear-to-ear grin announcing, "I did it!"

And, often, when you do figure out a successful way to respond to your child, she is moving on to a new developmental stage, raising new questions that require new decisions. Just as your child is learning and growing every day, so are you.

Of course, it's not possible (or even advisable) to stop to analyze everything you say and do. Yet when time and energy allow, trying to understand your feelings and reactions to the demands of parenting can help you make decisions that will make a positive difference for your child. We invite you to think about yourself as a parent for the following four reasons.

Knowing your goals for your child influences how you respond to him. Picture a toddler throwing puzzle pieces across the room. Parents will respond differently, based on their parenting goals. For example:

- A mother who wants to make sure that her child learns to follow rules and be well-behaved takes the puzzle away. She explains that puzzles are not for throwing and redirects the child to another toy.

- A father whose goal is to help his child better manage frustration explains that throwing puzzle pieces is not okay, encourages the child not to give up, and offers to help the child discover where the pieces might fit.

- A father who doesn't want his child to feel frustrated puts the puzzle pieces in their spaces for his child.

What do you think?
> *What might the child learn from each of these responses?*
> *How might you respond in this situation? Why?*
> *What are some of your goals for your child? How do they influence your daily decisions?*

Understanding some of the reasons behind what you do can help you rethink your decisions when things don't work out the way you had hoped. Renee is sick and tired of daily battles with her toddler, Shaniqua, over the clothing she chooses to wear. Renee wonders how she can change course. She thinks about why it is so important to her that Shaniqua be "put together." Renee realizes that her own mother was always very controlling about what she wore—wanting Renee to look "just right." Renee felt a lot of resentment about this control. With this realization and the recognition that Shaniqua is at an age where she wants and needs to assert her independence, Renee decides to handle things differently. She lets Shaniqua make her own choices—among options that Renee offers.

What do you think?

➤ *Have you been in a similar situation, when you felt an intense response to your child's behavior but were not sure why?*

➤ *What might be some of the reasons for your strong reaction?*

Being in tune with your own feelings and reactions helps you avoid jumping to conclusions and helps you consider different possible meanings of your child's behavior. A dad who is very particular about organization may see his 12-month-old as misbehaving when he takes every toy out of the toy chest. But he could also see his son's behavior as admirable perseverance in searching for a treasured toy. (In fact, being methodical is a trait that this father and son may have in common!) A mom who had lots of conflict with her older sister while growing up may see the typical sibling rivalry occurring between her 2-year-old twins as a serious problem in their relationship. This view may prompt her to (unnecessarily) run interference between the twins.

What do you think?

➤ *Did your child do something recently that concerned or annoyed you?*

➤ *Why do you think you reacted that way?*

➤ *What was your assumption about the meaning of this behavior? What are some other possible meanings?*

Knowing and accepting that your feelings count can help you make decisions that work for both you and your child. Feelings are not right or wrong. Sometimes, like all parents, you have tender, loving feelings about your child. At other times, your child may exhaust you, frustrate you, or get on your nerves. Being aware of how you are feeling can help you balance your needs with your child's and make decisions that work for both of you.

Self-Awareness: A Change of Mindset

One father of two children comments, "Do I have to quit my job to do this self-awareness thing? I don't have the time or energy for new projects these days." Few parents do. But self-awareness isn't another task to add to your already busy days. Rather, it is a change of mindset that helps you

• *pause for a moment,*

• *think about your feelings and where they come from, and*

• *make decisions based on your child's needs—and your own.*

On the way home from child care, Cordell pulls his father's hand toward the park where they often go. But today, Dad is tired. He didn't sleep well last night. Chasing Cordell around the park is the last thing he wants to do. His head throbs just thinking about it. Dad is also thinking about the busy weekend they have planned. He and Cordell's mom are divorced, and this is Dad's weekend to have Cordell. Dad knows that saying no to the park will really disappoint Cordell, but he takes his chances. "We'll go to the park tomorrow," he says. Cordell begins to whine. Dad thinks of something Cordell really likes to do at home. "I'll put the cover over the table and make a tent for you and your stuffed animals to play in. You can have a snack in there."

What do you think?
➤ **Think of a time you have been in a similar situation. How did you handle it?**
➤ **How did things turn out?**
➤ **What, if anything, might you do differently next time?**

Now we turn to three elements that you bring to parenthood—elements that influence who you are as a parent and the decisions that you make:

- Your hopes for your child.
- Your own childhood experiences.
- Your temperament.

Your Hopes (and Fears) for Your Child

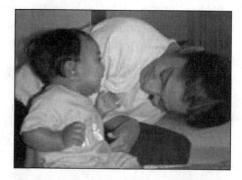

All parents have dreams for their child. You may dream that your child will be a gifted musician, teacher, athlete, or inventor. Parents also have fears. One dad worries that his child will have trouble in school, as he had. A mom fears that her son, who looks a lot like her brother, will turn out like him—a man with a drinking problem and a bad temper.

When you are aware of your hopes and fears, you will be better able to see your child for who she is and respond to her unique personality and interests. For example, you may have dreamed of a cuddly baby, but your daughter is a squirmer who is always on the move. Rather than try to convince her to sit with you in the rocking chair, you may decide to spend more time together on a blanket on the floor. Realizing that you hoped to be the parent of an athlete can help you see what your son really enjoys—playing with play dough and finger painting rather than climbing or running around. Of course, this preference doesn't mean that he will never set foot on an athletic field or that you should never encourage your child to chase and kick a ball. It simply means that, for now, your son is showing you what interests him, and by supporting your child's interests, you are showing your respect and love.

> *What do **you** think?*
> ➣ *Before your baby was born, what did you imagine she would be like? How is your child alike and how is she different from what you had hoped?*
> ➣ *What has been your biggest surprise in being a parent? Your greatest delight? Your biggest disappointment?*
> ➣ *How do you think your hopes and fears influence the way you see and respond to your child?*

Your Childhood Experiences

Two-month-old Natasha cries whenever she isn't being held. Her mother, Sherri, sees Natasha as too needy. Sherri feels smothered by and angry with her.

Two-month-old Brian cries whenever he isn't being held. His mother, Maria, quickly picks him up each time. Maria loves to feel needed. Even when Brian is sitting contentedly in his infant seat, she finds herself taking him out to hold him.

Why such different responses? Each of these mothers, like every parent, brings to parenting her own ideas, feelings, and expectations about parent–child relationships and the proper way to raise children. Each mother's response is based, in large part, on her own experiences growing up.

Going Home Again
How many times have you opened your mouth to say something and heard your parents' words? You're not alone. Most parents have had this experience. It helps you see how deeply you are influenced by childhood experiences and why it's so important to become aware of how they shape your approach to parenting today.

For better and worse, just as you are your child's first teacher, your parents were yours. Things they said and did, their way of being and relating to you and others, laid the foundation for many of your beliefs, values, attitudes, and parenting practices. Few parents, if any, had a lesson plan in mind. The transfer of information mostly took place through your everyday interactions with one another. You tuned in to the not-so-subtle and subtle messages they sent, which influenced how you thought about yourself and the world around you.

What do you think?
> *What were some of the messages you received as a child?*
> *What influence, if any, do you think these messages have on your parenting?*

Voices From the Past
Here are some messages that parents told us they received as kids:

- *Cleanliness is next to godliness.*
- *Children should be seen, not heard.*
- *You are only as good as your grades.*

Parents often re-create with their children what they experienced with their own parents. Sometimes it's done on purpose. For example, a dad decides to take his toddler out to splash in the puddles because this activity is something special he remembers doing with

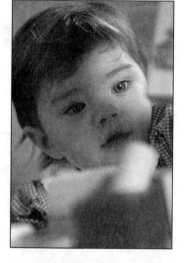

his dad. Some parents try to do the opposite of what their parents did. A mom decides never to insist that her child try a new food because her mother always forced her to do so. A dad tries to show his child a lot of physical affection because his own father rarely did.

Most likely, you sometimes "go home again"—act on beliefs, values, and experiences from your childhood—without making a conscious decision to do so. The amount of crying, fussing, and clinging that you can tolerate from your baby or toddler, the way you treat a boy compared with the way you treat a girl, the way you react to sibling rivalry, and your approach to discipline all may have roots in your early experience.

Sometimes, you will be able to uncover a link between a childhood experience and something you say or do. One father told us that he realized he was constantly protecting his younger son from his older son because he himself had been teased relentlessly by his older brother as a child. But at other times, the connection between past and present may not be so clear. When you are aware that you are having an intense reaction to something about your child, don't just do something, stand there! (Unless, of course, your child is in some kind of danger and you have to act immediately to keep him safe.) Stop and ask yourself where your feelings are coming from—or at least acknowledge that they may be out of proportion to the situation at hand. Then try to make a decision about how to respond based on what is happening in the moment, not on what happened in the past.

Thinking About Yesterday Can Help You With Decisions Today

If you grew up in a supportive, nurturing family, you may have learned by example many positive lessons about parenting. Trying to capture what these lessons meant to you and putting them into words can help you discover the origins of your own ways of supporting your child. If you grew up in a less-than-nurturing environment—for example, in a home where there was a lack of warmth and affection, constant arguing, neglect, or substance abuse—then self-awareness can help you avoid unintentionally re-creating the parenting patterns that are familiar but were hurtful to you as a child.

Let's look at how two parents, who love and want the best for their children, react differently to similar child behaviors.

Sandra really wants her child, Lexi (13 months), to be self-sufficient. When Lexi can't get the jack-in-the-box to pop up, Sandra watches, thinking it best to let Lexi figure it out on her own. Lexi finally gives up. A friend with whom she spends a lot of time asks Sandra why she is so "hard" on Lexi—why she expects so much of her and doesn't help her more. Sandra realizes she has never thought of it this way.

Alan wants his son, Jordan (13 months), to feel competent. When Jordan can't make the jack-in-the-box pop up, Alan quickly runs over to turn the crank. He can't bear to see his son fail. Recently, Alan has noticed that Jordan gives up more easily than many of the other children in his playgroup; he immediately looks for help before trying to solve a problem on his own. Alan wonders whether Jordan's behavior may have something to do with his own readiness to jump in.

Wondering about the possible reasons for their reactions helps these parents reconsider their choices—and make new ones if necessary.

Sandra makes a connection between her reactions to Lexi and the fact that her own single mother instilled a strong sense in Sandra and her three sisters that being independent and doing for themselves—not depending on others—was very important. Sandra realizes that her mother may have insisted on self-reliance because she had little support in caring for four young girls and wanted to teach them to be self-sufficient. Sandra has enormous respect for her mother but recognizes that her own situation is different. Sandra's partner, Ruth, is very involved in helping care for Lexi. Sandra also has support from other moms in the neighborhood. She is learning that it's okay to rely on others and that giving Lexi more support and nurturing won't keep her from growing up to be capable and strong.

My mother died when I was 10. I grew up feeling very alone. Now that I have a child of my own, I find it very hard to separate from her or let her cry or struggle at all. I feel anxious anytime she is not with me. I think this has a lot to do with the loss of my mom.

Alan, Jordan's dad, recognizes that his need to rescue Jordan from every struggle may have something to do with his experience growing up. His father believed that letting children struggle on their own built character. Alan felt incompetent much of the time—as if he couldn't master anything. But now, Alan begins to question whether trying to do the opposite of what his own father did is really helping to nurture Jordan's self-confidence. He decides to try a new strategy. Rather than jump in so quickly and solve problems for Jordan, Alan decides to become his son's coach. Alan guides Jordan as he struggles to solve problems for himself. He believes that this approach may help Jordan feel competent in a way that Alan never did.

*What do **you** think?*

> *How did your mother, father, or other loved ones help you to feel good about yourself and your abilities? What did they do and say? What do you do to help your child feel good about herself?*

> *Were there ways your family members made you feel bad about yourself? What did they do and say? Do you do or say anything to your own child that is similar? Different?*

> *What were some significant events or experiences in your childhood (for example, a move, the loss of a loved one, the birth of a sibling)? How do you think these experiences influence you as a parent?*

> ### The Past Is in the Present
> My husband and I were in total disagreement about our expectations for our 20-month-old daughter, Emily, at dinnertime. He felt that she should stay in her high chair until we were all done, that she should not be allowed to get down and play or sit on my lap after she was finished eating. This behavior seemed way too much to expect from a 20-month-old. I couldn't understand why he was so concerned with her table manners. Then, as we were each arguing our point of view, he told me that his parents often tell a story about taking him to a fancy restaurant when he was 4. He was so well behaved that the maitre d' gave him a bag of candy. I began to understand where his expectations might be coming from.

Your Temperament

Many researchers think of temperament as the typical ways in which a person reacts to the world and the strategies she uses to manage her reactions. Temperament expresses itself in many ways. Some people tend to be slow to warm up to new places and people. Others eagerly jump into new situations. Some people have intense reactions, experiencing and expressing their feelings in a big way. They are either ecstatic or enraged. Others are more laid back, taking things in stride. Keep in mind that temperament describes a person's inborn general tendencies, her typical responses. A person with a cautious temperament isn't always fearful when faced with something new. Likewise, a person with an outgoing temperament might sometimes feel cautious or shy.

Your temperament influences who and how you are as a parent. If you are a very active parent who has a child who loves to sit and explore quietly, then recognizing and respecting your differences will help you separate your needs from your child's. This process will help you understand, accept, and appreciate your child for who he is.

> *Kevin is a very active, outgoing person who loves to try new things. Today, he has taken his 11-month-old daughter, Tyra, to the park for the first time. Tyra is playing alone in the sandbox when a group of toddlers joins her. At first, Tyra smiles and eagerly watches their play. But as the toddlers become more active and noisy, Tyra's smiles turn quickly to tears. She starts to crawl out of the sandbox and reach for Kevin, who picks her up and comforts her. But then Kevin goes a step further. After Tyra calms down, Kevin gently encourages her to play near the other children. He sits at her side, talking and playing with her. Soon Tyra is slowly creeping closer to the group of toddlers, curiously watching their moves.*

Kevin's decision about how to respond to a daughter with a temperament very different from his has a powerful influence on what Tyra learns from this experience. Kevin lets Tyra know that he understands her and that her needs and feelings are important. At the same time, he uses his own comfort with and need for social interaction to help Tyra manage a challenging situation and to expand her world. Rather than just take her away from the sandbox, he provides the support necessary for her to feel comfortable so she can continue playing. His response may also help Tyra adapt to and feel confident to handle other challenges as she grows. (Chapter 3 will explore how you and your child "fit" together in greater depth.)

> **What do you think?**
> ➤ *Have you ever been in a situation like Kevin's where you used your own strengths to help your child handle a difficult situation? What happened?*
> ➤ *What effect do you think your response had on your child?*

Knowing Your Limits and Limitations

Whether they work outside or inside the home, most parents of young children that we talk to tell us that, on most days, they don't feel as though they have accomplished nearly what they had hoped or expected. A mom who is trying to comfort her inconsolable baby doesn't ask for help and won't put the baby down in a safe place for just a few minutes because she feels that these actions would be signs of her incompetence. Another mom, who feels that she should be able to work all day, do errands on the way home, and make a three-course dinner for her family, feels so physically drained that she is unable to play with and enjoy her child during their evening time together. Acknowledging all that you do—and that you can't be perfect—is important. Your expectations of yourself shape the decisions that you make for your child.

I used to get so much done when I was working. I'm blown away now by the fact that when I am home all day with the baby, I can barely keep the house clean or make dinner.

I literally spent an entire day comforting my sick 5-month-old, Sara—trying to get her to sleep and all that stuff you do to make babies feel better. I never even took a shower. At first glance I thought I had done a whole lot of nothing that day. It wasn't until my wife called from work to ask how Sara was that I realized I was doing something incredibly important.

You Do Much More Than You Think

When we have asked parents to review everything they did in all—or even part—of a day, they have been amazed to see all they had done. Choose a day or part of a day—for example, from the time you wake up in the morning until you leave the house for work or, if you are home, until lunchtime. Think about or make notes of everything you do during this time period.

What do you think?

➤ *What may your child have learned from some of the things you did with or for him?*

➤ *What did you learn about your child?*

➤ *What moments made you laugh? What moments made your child laugh?*

➤ *What was your favorite moment? Why?*

➤ *What do you think was your child's favorite moment? Why?*

➤ *How might you shift your priorities and expectations to make decisions that will increase the number of those moments that you treasure most?*

Nobody's Perfect—And You Don't Have To Be

Rebecca put her 5-month-old, Jessie, in her crib for a nap and went out on the porch to relax and read the newspaper, only to find out 15 minutes later that the monitor wasn't working and her baby had been crying. "There goes the mother–child bond," she despaired.

Knowing and respecting your limits also means recognizing that nobody, including you, is perfect and that nobody makes the best decisions all the time.

Have no fear: No single mistake will scar your child for life. It is the accumulation of your interactions with your child that counts. (And you can be sure that your child will give you many chances to try again!) In fact, "mistakes" often create the best learning opportunities. It's all about trial and error.

<u>Two Busy Moms</u>

The Single-Mom Shuffle

Here is the list made by a single working mother of a 5-month-old girl. Her list covers 5½ hours—from when she picks up her daughter at child care until she (the mother) goes to sleep at night.

5:00—Drive to child care to pick up Maddie.

5:30—Arrive home and fix Maddie a bowl of cereal.

6:00—Drive to grocery store for more diapers.

6:30—Cook dinner while Maddie swings.

7:00—Hold Maddie in my arms while eating dinner.

7:30—Give Maddie a bath.

8:00—Nurse Maddie until she falls asleep. Do the dishes, straighten up the kitchen, feed the dog and cats, trot down to the basement to start one load of laundry (including all the dirty bibs), let the dog out into the backyard, and troubleshoot the network connection on the computer.

9:00—When Maddie wakes up, carry her around for a while, then rock her in the rocking chair. Hear the dog barking and let him in.

9:30—Put Maddie back in her crib. Do 20 minutes of exercise and stretching while watching TV.

10:00—Take a quick shower.

10:15—Snack before bed.

10:30—Get into bed. Read for 15 minutes before passing out.

Morning Minuet

Here are the notes from a part-time working mother of 2-month-old Haley and 5-year-old Sydney.

4:45 a.m.

Haley has woken up for the third time since 1:00 a.m. She is hungry and very fidgety. She eagerly sucks her bottle but keeps her eyes tightly shut. Maybe she's actually starting to switch her nights and days around. Relief is in sight! What a nice thought at this hour, despite how much I enjoy the privacy of our nightly feedings.

7:15–8:30 a.m.

Sydney is still sleeping and my husband has already left for work. I am having coffee and giving Haley her breakfast bottle. This is a favorite time of ours because she is rested and very animated and happy. As she sweetly chats away and smiles, she notices her hand. She pulls it to her mouth and begins to suck. What an accomplishment! I am so proud of her. She seems so delighted with herself.

With Haley in my arms, I make Sydney's lunch. I then go upstairs, change Haley's diaper, and get her dressed. I wake Sydney up, help her pick out her outfit, watch her get dressed for school and brush her hair and teeth. I make breakfast for Sydney and sit and talk with her as she eats. Then I feed the cat. I have done all of this while still holding Haley.

I put Haley down while I put on my gym clothes. Then I get the girls in the car to take Sydney to school.

9:00 a.m.

Haley has dozed off. I drop her off at the child-care center at the gym, and she immediately wakes up. She calls for someone to pick her up so she can look at the other children in the center. She is getting so alert that she no longer wants to sleep when she is in an exciting, new place.

9:45 a.m.

Run to the coffeeshop, glance through paper for 10 minutes. Give Haley another bottle and change her diaper.

10:00 a.m.

Go to the grocery store for a few items. I feed Haley a bottle with one hand and shop with the other.

10:45 am

Home again, I try to answer work e-mails with Haley curled up asleep on my lap.

Trial and Error

I was having the hardest time helping my 18-month-old, Sharif, to calm down. I tried everything I could think of—talking to him, holding him, offering to read his favorite book—but it seemed that the harder I tried, the more upset he got. One day, I just threw up my hands and, feeling terrible and helpless, walked away, leaving Sharif alone in his room. Believe it or not, within 5 minutes, I heard him stop crying. I peeked into his room and saw that he was happily looking at some books and talking to his stuffed animals. I couldn't believe it. What he really needed all along was to be left alone! I learned that day that when Sharif is losing it, he needs some space to calm down on his own. Who would have thought? I told Sharif's child-care provider about this discovery which has made her job easier and Sharif a lot happier!

Everyone Needs Support

Caring for a young child requires a tremendous amount of emotional and physical energy. But knowing when to ask for support and giving yourself permission to ask for it doesn't always come easily. It might mean deciding to ask a spouse, partner, friend, or neighbor whom you trust to watch the baby while you take a well-deserved break. It might mean deciding to walk to visit a friend after asking a relative or a sitter you trust to come over and "share the care" during the late afternoon or early evening. Another option is calling or visiting a parent support center in your community.

What do you think?

> *At what time of day is your child the most calm, content, and engaged? When is he fussiest?*

> *When are you most calm? Fussiest?*

> *How do you know when you need a break?*

> *What can you do to have more of the times you enjoy and fewer of those that are stressful? What tasks could you give up? Delegate? In what ways could you change your routine—for example, filling the bottom of a closet with extra packages of diapers to avoid last-minute races to the store?*

> *To do your best as a parent, what kind of help do you need from others? Who can you call for support?*

Break Time

"At times, it's all about survival," says a new mother with a deep sigh. This perspective brings up another important aspect of knowing your limits—recognizing when your frustration or anger is building and you need to step out of the action to catch your breath. "Survival" may mean deciding to put an inconsolable child somewhere safe, such as a crib, and taking a brief break, or it may mean calling a friend to let off steam. Both you and your child will benefit.

Before we consider step 2 in the decision-making process—tuning in to your child—remember that a key part of meeting your child's needs is fulfilling some of your own personal needs. Making decisions that will accommodate your needs and your child's can be tough. Most parents are inclined to let their own needs slide as they attempt to do everything and be everything for their children.

But parents need some time for themselves. Taking care of yourself—physically, emotionally, and spiritually—and taking care of the important relationships in your life—with your spouse, partner, friends, and family—is crucial for your child's healthy development. When you feel nurtured, you have more to give your child. And as your child grows, you are showing her the importance of loving relationships. So try to make time, whenever you can, to take care of your own needs—whether that means exercising, going to a ball game, visiting an elderly relative, reading, seeing a movie, or having coffee with a friend.

The first time I spent a whole day away from my son, someone asked whether I missed him. I answered honestly, "No," and then wondered whether that was an acceptable response.

*What do **you** think?*
> *Do you take time for yourself? What do you do to care for yourself?*
> *What do you wish that you had more time to do? How can you make time for it?*

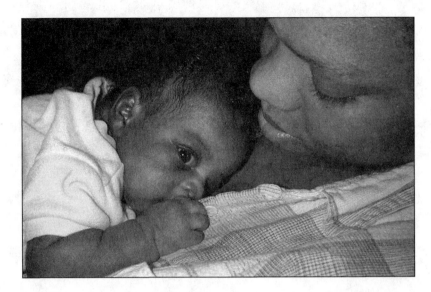

Remember—

• The things you say and do, the decisions you make every day as you dress your child, eat breakfast together, play, and set limits, shape how she develops and who she becomes.

• When time and energy allow, trying to understand your feelings and reactions can help you proceed in new ways and make decisions about how to respond that will make a positive difference for your child.

• When you are aware that you are having an intense reaction to something about your child, don't just do something, stand there. Think of the reaction as a signal that perhaps something in your past experience is influencing you. Take some time to reflect before you respond—unless your child is in danger.

• Know and respect your limits. Recognize that nobody, including you, is perfect, and that nobody makes the right decisions all the time.

• Take care of yourself and the important relationships in your life. This step is crucial for your child's healthy development

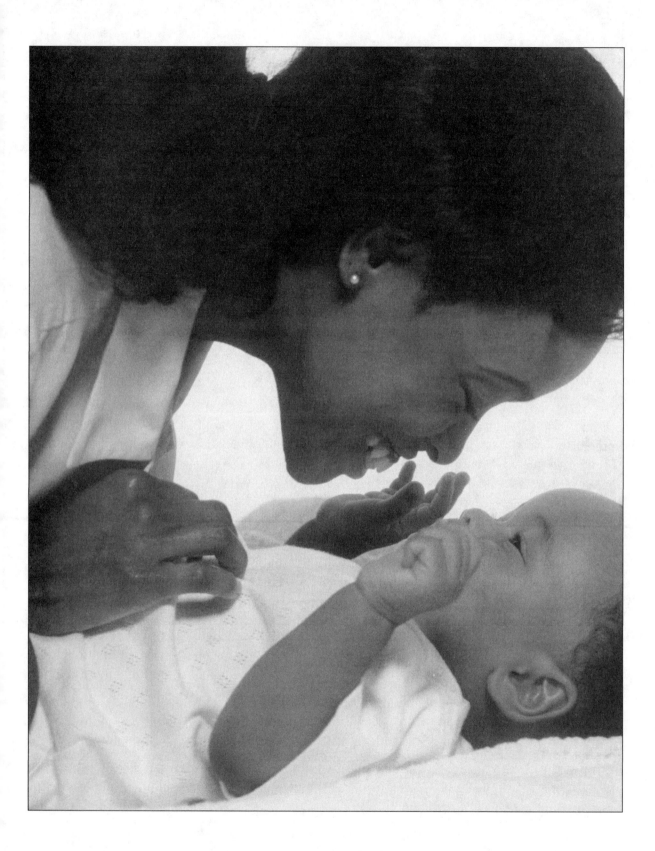

CHAPTER 2
Step 2: Tune in to Your Child

THIS CHAPTER EXPLORES STEP 2 in the decision-making process—understanding and appreciating your child.

Reading Your Child's Cues: Looking From the Outside to Understand What's Happening on the Inside

Understanding your child means taking the time to tune in to what he is "telling" you. Young children haven't yet learned to hide what is going on inside of them (a skill some of us adults have developed a little too well!). Much of what they think and feel is expressed through their sounds, gestures, words, facial expressions, and actions. Therefore, watching what they do on the "outside" gives you important clues about what is happening on the inside. Like a detective, you look for clues and try to figure out how they fit together and what they mean. Then you decide what more you need to find out to put together the pieces of the puzzle that are your child's behavior.

Putting the Pieces Together

What you might observe	What a child might be telling you
Four-month-old Ryan fingers the silky edge of the blanket in his crib, then flings out his arms, pushing the blanket aside. He waves his arms in the air and then touches his hands together.	These hands belong to me! I can control how they move and what they do.
Fifteen-month-old Tasha points to the bookshelf. Her mom takes down a book. Tasha shouts "No!" and throws it on the floor.	You got it wrong! That's not the one I wanted! or No! I wanted to get it myself!
Two-year-old Jake is telling his stuffed giraffe, "I have to go now but I will be back. Don't cry. Elephant will play with you."	Separations are hard for me. I am working on managing those feelings by playing a game where I get to be the one who leaves.

What do you think?
> *Observe your child during a daily routine such as eating or dressing or as she plays. What do you think she is thinking? Feeling?*

You Observe All the Time

You observe every day when you see or hear something—or don't see or hear something—and you use this information to figure out what another person might be feeling or thinking inside. For example:

- You assume your spouse had a tough day at work when you hear the flat tone of her "hello" while walking in the door.

- You take a walk with a friend and sense that something is bothering him when he continually looks down and is more quiet than usual.

- You see your child's lips purse and her arms tense while trying to get on a shoe, and you figure that your child has reached her limit of frustration.

- You suspect that your toddler and his friend are up to some kind of mischief when, suddenly, they are silent and you hear no squabbling or crying.

- You see your child rubbing her eyes and tugging on her left ear, and you think it's time to put away the blocks and head upstairs to get ready for bed.

Take Time To Wonder

The same behavior in a child can mean many different things. Waking during the middle of the night may be caused by separation anxiety, difficulty with self-soothing, a new crib, illness, or many other reasons. A toddler's tantrum can be brought on by countless factors, such as fatigue, hunger, frustration, or anger that you said no to a cookie before dinner. Taking time to wonder about what your child's behavior is telling you will help you make better decisions. And recognize that finding the best response often entails a process of trial and error.

You will not always be able to figure out what your child is telling you. No matter how good a detective you are or how many clues your observations yield, you can't always

Rebecca is feeding her 14-month-old daughter, Ella, some applesauce. Ella pushes the spoon away and cries, "No!" Rebecca offers another spoonful, and Ella again rejects it. Rebecca decides this means that Ella, who loves applesauce, is just not hungry, so she takes away the bowl. Ella begins to scream and bang on the high chair. Now Rebecca thinks, "Okay, so you are hungry," and spoons up more applesauce. Again, rejection. Applesauce goes flying onto the floor, and Ella bursts into what Rebecca describes as "enraged sobs." Ella shouts, "No, no, no, no, no!" Rebecca is thinking about the sticky mess on the floor and is working hard not to be angry. And she is incredibly frustrated about not knowing what Ella wants. She wonders out loud, "Maybe you want to feed yourself." She decides to find out. "Okay. Here's the spoon." Ella immediately quiets down, smiles with satisfaction, grabs the spoon, and begins to feed herself.

solve the mystery of why your child is acting clingy or cranky or is suddenly afraid of the dark. In these instances, Lynnette, mother of 11-month-old Lucca, wisely advises, "You just ride the wave and tell yourself 'this too shall pass.'"

As you embark on your "investigations," you might ask yourself some of the following key questions (also shown in the box on this page). They can help you avoid jumping to conclusions and can turn everyday watching into a rich source of information to help you read your child's cues accurately and make good decisions about how to respond. Sample responses appear in parentheses.

- **What did I observe?** (I saw my 33-month-old son, Johnny, chase another toddler, Alex, and then pull on the back of Alex's shirt.)

- **Where did it take place?** (On the playground.)

- **What else was going on? What happened right before? Right after?** (Lots of kids were playing tag together. Johnny wasn't part of the group, but he was watching. Then Johnny started to chase Alex, but Alex paid no attention to him. Johnny pulled on Alex's shirt. Alex yelled, "Stop!" and ran away from Johnny, returning to the game. Johnny sat down by himself, looking very sad.)

> **Key Questions**
>
> *What did I observe?*
>
> *Where did it take place?*
>
> *What else was going on? What happened right before? Right after?*
>
> *What might my child's behavior be saying? (You may have several guesses.)*
>
> *How should I respond?*
>
> *What can I learn from my child's reaction to my response?*

- **What might my child's behavior be saying?** (You may have several guesses, such as Johnny was just being "bad;" Johnny felt left out and was taking it out on Alex; or Johnny wanted to play with Alex and was trying to get his attention.)

- **How should I respond?** (I think that Johnny was misbehaving. I have seen him be too rough with other kids like this many times before. I made him sit in time-out for a few minutes, during which time Johnny kept insisting that he just wanted to play tag and that no one was listening to him or letting him play.)

- **What can I learn from my child's reaction to my response?** (As I listened to Johnny's explanation, I felt that he wasn't being hurtful on purpose. I wonder whether this behavior is the only way he knows to get other kids' attention. I think that the next time we are around other kids, I will watch more carefully to see just how things unfold. Maybe I'll also plan some playdates. If and when I see Johnny getting too rough, I can try to help him find other ways to play without annoying or hurting someone.)

Understanding Your Child's Behavior

The following three key pieces will help you put together the whole puzzle:

- **Context:** What is going on in your child's world? For example, has she experienced a recent move? A favorite aunt coming for a visit? The arrival of a new baby? Parents who are stressed and arguing a lot? The return of a parent from a business trip? The loss of a family pet? Where is your child and with whom is she interacting when the behavior takes place? Is your child with a friend, caregiver, grandma? Is she at child care, at a friend's home, in the grocery store?

- **Developmental age and stage:** Where is your child, developmentally? Knowing what to expect at each stage of your child's development is essential for under-standing his behavior. For example, if your 6-month-old, who used to go to any-one, now cries when someone new reaches out to him, he may have reached a developmental milestone—the ability to tell the difference between a familiar person and a stranger. If your 2-year-old starts to wake up in the middle of the night, he may be having nightmares that often start around this age. (For more information on early development, see Appendix A.)

- **Temperament:** What is your child's personal style and approach to the world? You can get to know your child's temperament by looking at the intensity of her reactions, how persistent she is, her activity level, how she reacts to new people, and how she responds to change.

Consider the following example to see how these pieces—context, developmental age and stage, and temperament—affect behavior.

Nine-month-old Jenna moved 3 weeks ago from the family child-care home (where she had been since she was 3 months old) to a high-quality child-care center. Her dad changed jobs, and the center is much closer to his new office. Since the change, Jenna has been very upset every morning when her father says good-bye. Jenna's new caregivers also report that she has a hard time napping, although she used to nap regularly in the family child-care home. Not getting the rest she needs has made her irritable in the afternoons. She just wants to be held by the caregiver she likes best.

Jenna's current situation—moving to a new child-care setting—is a big change for any child, especially for one who is somewhat fearful and cautious in new situations. In addition, her dad has just changed jobs, and Jenna may be sensing his anxiety. Thus, we can see that *context* plays a key role in determining Jenna's behavior. In terms of *development*, Jenna is beginning to understand that people and things she can't see still exist. She may protest at her dad's departure, in part because she now can picture him even after he leaves and hopes she can make him come back. (In fact, she may have reacted the very same way to her dad's departure had she still been in her family child-care home.) Jenna's *temperament* also drives her behavior. Jenna's parents know that she needs time to adapt to new people and situations, but with time and support, she usually adjusts well. So she will need some time to feel safe and comfortable in the new center.

Jenna is also particularly sensitive to sounds. For example, her parents have noticed that, when they turn the volume up on the stereo, Jenna will immediately turn to look at the speakers, and she sometimes cries if it is too loud. This sensitivity may explain why she is having a hard time napping. Although the new center has a separate room for napping, as did the family child care, the new room is right next to the classroom, so it is much noisier.

Considering all these factors can help Jenna's parents and caregivers understand her behavior and decide how best to respond. For example, knowing that Jenna needs time to adjust to new situations can lead her caregivers to offer more support and not expect that she will interact fully until she feels more comfortable. Dad might stay for a few minutes at drop-off to help Jenna make the transition, perhaps by reading her a story along with a caregiver. And being aware of Jenna's sensitivity to noise, her caregivers can try to arrange for Jenna to nap in a quieter area.

Now, let's take a closer look at each of these pieces of the puzzle. You will see that, together, these pieces help you create a picture of your child in a certain time and place.

Context

We begin with context because it is the backdrop for each of the other factors. The following questions can help you look at the world through your child's eyes and think about what may be influencing her behavior:

- How is your child's health? Has she been sick recently?
- What's happening with daily routines? Have there been any changes in her schedule?

- What is going on with other family members? (For example, is anyone celebrating a recent success or under an unusual amount of stress? If there are two parents or other adults in the household, how is their relationship? Is there a sibling who has been ill or who is needing extra attention at this time?)

- Have there been other recent changes (for example, a move, a loss in the family, a visiting relative, a new sibling)?

- Who is with your child when the behavior occurs? Where does the behavior take place?

Developmental Age and Stage

The first 3 years are a time of incredible development. From the day they are born, babies are ready and eager to learn. No one has to tell babies to practice crawling, or babbling, or filling up and dumping out. They are driven to learn new skills and master challenges. By the time children are 3, they have learned to dress and feed themselves, to walk, to dance, to talk, to sing, to imagine, to give and accept love, to be confident and secure, to show empathy, to be curious, and much, much more. The development that occurs in the early years lays the foundation for a lifetime of learning and relationships. As you watch your child grow, the following factors will be helpful to keep in mind.

Although development in the early years generally follows a predictable course—for example, most children crawl before they walk—there is great variation in how and when children master developmental milestones and learn new skills. Consider this scenario: Two babies are presented with a pop-up toy. One baby, who loves to move, may be so busy crawling and climbing that he doesn't spend much time working on the fine-motor (finger) skills necessary to get the animals to appear. The other baby, who loves to explore with his hands, can make a favorite doggie pop up long before focusing energy on crawling. Also keep in mind that when children master a new skill, there is often some backward movement in other areas; for example, a child who has just learned to walk may act more clingy than usual.

Each area of development—intellectual, social, emotional, motor, and language—depends on and influences other areas. Think about the 9-month-old who is lifting both arms to tell her dad that she "wants up." This apparently simple gesture is, in fact, very complex. It begins with the baby's desire to be picked up and held. This desire is an indication of her social and emotional development. The baby has formed a close, trusting relationship with her father; she knows that she can count on him to care for her. Her intellectual development is revealed by the fact that she has figured out a way to communicate her desires: If I lift up my arms, he'll know that I want him to pick me up. Finally, she has to have the physical coordination—the motor development—to be able to stretch her arms up in the right direction and send her message.

Dramatic brain development in the early years establishes patterns for lifelong learning. Thanks to new technology, brain researchers can see just how complex and active a young child's brain is. We now know, for example, that a range of early experiences affects how the brain functions. Those parts of your baby's brain concerned with language are being shaped as he listens to you coo and talk—long before he utters his first word. Parts of the brain that will eventually enable your child to walk are being fired up when, as a newborn, he waves his arms and legs randomly in the air.

You help your baby's healthy brain development when you respond sensitively to what she is "telling" you. For example, babies can sometimes get overloaded. When your baby turns her eyes or body away, arches her back, or even hiccups, she may be telling you that she needs a break from play, from specific sights or sounds, or from too many people around. When you sensitively read and respond to your baby's signals, for example, by lowering your voice, stopping a game, or turning down the music, you will help her relax and feel content. She can then focus attention on her most important job—learning about the surrounding world at her own pace. Your sensitive, responsive caregiving and interactions with your baby are more important to her development than any toy (despite toy companies' claims that their new toys will "make your baby smarter"). What you are already doing in your everyday activities and interactions with your child are all the "brain exercises" she needs.

Temperament: What Is Your Child's Personal Style?

Every child is born with his own individual way of approaching the world—a temperament. Temperament is not something that he chooses, nor is it something that you create. A child's temperament shapes the way he experiences the world. A child who is cautious and needs time to feel comfortable in new situations and a child who jumps right in are likely to have very different experiences going to a birthday party or a new school. A child who can handle a lot of sensory stimulation will experience a trip to the supermarket differently from a child who has a low threshold for a lot of surrounding noise and action.

Look at how three 27-month-old boys—Rahim, Frank, and Carlos—enter a new classroom in a child-care center. The boys' behavior suggests the powerful effect that temperament has on a child's experience.

In one corner of the classroom is a group of tables with puzzles and art supplies. A climbing gym dominates another corner of the room. A third corner contains a large mirror with all kinds of dress-up paraphernalia hanging within a toddler's reach. In the center of the room, five toddlers are working together to build towers and roadways as part of an elaborate block structure.

Rahim and his mother open the door and scan the room. Within moments of entering, Rahim rips off his coat and abandons his mom to join the children building with the blocks. He takes a block in his hand and sits down. "Make it big," one of the builders instructs Rahim. "This big," Rahim says, eagerly, reaching above his head.

Children like Rahim generally approach new situations and new people easily. They have an easy time with transitions and meeting new people, and are often described as kids who "go with the flow."

When Frank and his dad arrive at the classroom, Frank spends a long time leaning into his dad's leg and refuses to take off his coat. After watching the other kids for a while, he inches away from his dad to get a closer look at a table where kids are working on puzzles. He returns to his dad's leg but soon inches away again—this time, toward the climbing gym. He lingers there before pulling off his coat and bringing it to his dad to hold. Frank then takes his dad's hand, and they walk back to the puzzle table. Frank sits down next to another child and gets to work.

Children like Frank are often cautious when facing unfamiliar terrain. Transitions can be hard for them. They need support and time to feel safe and comfortable. At the same time, these children often enjoy playing quietly on their own or with just one or two friends. They typically don't need a lot of "entertainment."

Carlos speeds into the room ahead of his grandmother—no time to waste looking around to check out what's going on. He charges up to two boys who are crawling on the floor, pushing fire trucks, and making siren sounds. Carlos grabs one of the trucks and yells, "MINE!"

Children like Carlos tend to be "big reactors." They seem to take in stimulation and respond intensely. They are quite passionate and can have difficulty controlling their strong feelings and desires. They jump for joy when they are happy and fume when they're not. They can be incredibly fun to be with because their excitement and passion are contagious.

Parents usually have a sense of their child's temperament. Rahim's mother wasn't surprised at his easy transition to child care: "It never takes him long to dive in." Frank's dad wasn't worried about his son eventually finding a comfortable place for himself in the room. He knew that Frank would eventually adjust—he just wasn't sure if it would take several minutes or several hours! Carlos's grandmother knew that her grandson would make his presence known in his new classroom. She recognizes how intense and strong-willed he is: "He knows what he wants and doesn't let anything get in his way." She is sometimes a bit overwhelmed and embarrassed by Carlos's intensity. At other times, she admires him and is proud of this trait—for example, when he throws himself into an art project or a ball game with his whole heart and soul.

As you think about your own child's temperament, keep the following points in mind.

Recognizing patterns in your child's behavior that are influenced by temperament can help you anticipate your child's responses to certain situations. If you know that your child has a hard time making transitions, you can guess that pick-up time at child care might be challenging. You could share this observation with your child's teacher and talk about how you can work together to make the end of the day easier. For example, the teacher can give your child a reminder that it will soon be time to go home. You might choose to spend a few minutes helping your child finish what she is doing, talk to your child's teachers at pick-up time, or bring along a snack and favorite book for your child to look at on the ride home.

> *What do* you *think?*
> ➤ *Do you see patterns in your child's behavior?*
> ➤ *How can you use this information to support your child?*

The way that children take in sensory experiences has a big influence on how they approach and experience the world. A baby who craves a lot of movement is often highly active. A child who is easily overwhelmed by too much surrounding noise and activity moves into new situations with caution and wants to interact with others only one at a time. A toddler who is very sensitive to being touched has intense reactions when anyone gets too close, especially when other children begin to push or bite.

Children have preferences for one sense over the other. One baby might scan a room carefully with his eyes, focusing on details like the flowers on the wallpaper or the reflection of light off your eyeglasses. Another is more tuned in to all kinds of sounds, from the squeak of a door to a tidbit of conversation. Still another is most interested in reaching out to touch things and, as soon as he is able, brings them to his mouth to explore with lips, gums, teeth, and tongue.

As you think about how your child uses her senses, remember that preferences can change; for example, a child who seems especially focused on mouthing or touching everything at one stage may become more interested in exploring by watching or listening later on.

What do you think?
> *How does your child use her senses? What are her preferences?*
> *How does the way your child takes in sensory experiences influence her behavior?*

Children can adapt. A child's behavior and approach to the world are shaped by his experiences and especially by his interactions with you. For example, children who are temperamentally shy can become more outgoing and comfortable in new situations when their parents help them sensitively and slowly adapt to new experiences.

Also, no matter how consistent a child's patterns may appear to be, sometimes children can—and will—catch you off guard by acting in ways that you do not expect. A child who is usually wary of strangers might fall madly in love with her new teacher. The fact that your child can surprise you is one of the most exciting and even delightful rewards of parenthood.

What do you think?
> *Has your child surprised you lately by acting in a way that you didn't expect? What happened?*
> *Think of a time you helped your child adapt or cope with a challenging situation. What did you do? How did it help your child?*

Culture matters. Different cultures place different values on behavioral styles. For example, some cultures value children who are quiet and obedient. Others value feisty, assertive kids. One dad, who lives in the inner city, expressed worry that his son was too laid back and not assertive or tough enough. He was afraid that his child would get bullied and taken advantage of by others.

> *What do you think?*
> ➤ *What are some of your cultural values around child rearing?*
> ➤ *How do you think they may shape how you see your child's behavior?*

There is no right or wrong, no better or worse temperament (although some are, no doubt, more challenging to handle). It's very important for children to be accepted for who they are. But let's face it, any parent with an intense, reactive child or a child who is very shy and slow to warm up will tell you that parenting these children can be hard. Stefanie, the mother of 2-year-old Danielle, described how she had moved to a new neighborhood and was desperate to meet some other moms. Finally, one day, a mom walked by with her very happy toddler who eagerly sought out Danielle and even offered to share her snack. Danielle, a slow-to-warm-up and intense child, pushed the bag away and then threw a huge tantrum when Stefanie tried to encourage her to play nicely. Stefanie later told her husband that Danielle was going to ruin her social life. (Of note is that Stefanie also describes Danielle as incredibly creative, smart, and passionate.)

Most parents prefer some of their child's temperamental characteristics to others.
Frank's father feels his patience dwindling and wishes that Frank was the kind of kid who would just get on with it rather than take so long to settle in. Carlos's mother sometimes wishes for a disappearing pill, like the day Carlos's exuberant hug knocked over a friend who hit his head on a chair as he fell down. Even Rahim's parents, who you may think have it made, at times wish Rahim were more assertive—for example, not letting everyone cut in front of him for a turn on the swing.

Parents struggle with these kinds of feelings for a range of reasons. Your child's behavior may remind you of parts of yourself that you don't like so much and want to change—like being easily hurt by other's unkindness. Conversely, you may feel discomfort with ways in which your child is very different from you—such as her ease and comfort in new situations when you like to take things slow. It is inevitable that you will like and feel more comfortable with some aspects of your child's temperament than with others.

A child's temperament influences how others respond to her. Keep in mind that children who are more irritable, intense, and feisty often meet with negative reactions from those around them. And it seems that, although these children cope much better when they have consistent limit setting, warmth, affection, and help regulating their strong emotions, parents and other caregivers find that providing this support for them is hard to do. In contrast, children who are shy often get no reaction at all from others, or they may be pressured to join in activities when, ideally, they need more time to stand back and watch.

Be Your Child's Champion

Have you ever found yourself feeling isolated from or misunderstood—even put down—by family, friends, and neighbors who disapprove of or judge your child? You are not alone.

A helpful approach is to see those situations as opportunities to educate others about your child. For example, a father explains to his aunt, who is not getting the warm reaction she wants from her niece, "Sophie, like a lot of other kids, needs time to adjust to new people." Dad then hands his aunt Sophie's favorite book, helping his aunt learn to approach Sophie slowly. You can also help others see your child's behavior from a different perspective. Here's how a mom describes her daughter, Tess, to a neighbor who is critical of Tess's feisty nature. "Tess knows who she is and what she wants. She is loving and she is fierce. She puts her whole heart into everything."

*What do **you** think?*
> *How do you see others responding to your child?*
> *How do you think your child's temperament may influence how people respond to him?*

Siblings can be (and often are) temperamentally very different. One mother told us, "In our house, we have two kids, and we parent them in two different ways."

*What do **you** think?*
> *If you have more than one child, how are they alike? How are they different?*
> *How do you adapt your parenting style to meet each of their needs?*

Five Temperament Characteristics

Your child's approach to the world is influenced by many factors. To help you put together a picture of your "whole child," we describe and explore the following characteristics to help you identify your child's way of approaching the world:

- Intensity of reaction
- Activity level
- Frustration tolerance
- Reaction to new people
- Reaction to change

As you read about these characteristics, picture temperament as a continuum. We describe what the characteristics look like on each end of their range, but you will see from the parent observations in each section that most children fall somewhere in between.

We also offer some ideas that you may decide to try as you parent a child with certain temperament characteristics. Adapt and use these suggestions on the basis of how you see your child's strengths and where he might need support. The goal isn't to change your child's temperament, but like most parents, you may find situations where you decide it would help if your child were more flexible, more willing to try something new, or more persistent. The suggestions can guide you in slowly and sensitively helping your child adapt to and even expand his world—for example, by helping a child who gets easily overwhelmed by sights and sounds feel comfortable in a new playgroup, encouraging a child who is low on patience to keep trying, or helping a reactive child learn to manage strong emotions so he doesn't overwhelm the other children and can make friends. You may also find that many of these suggestions, although offered as responses to a specific temperament characteristic, are also useful for many parenting situations that you encounter.

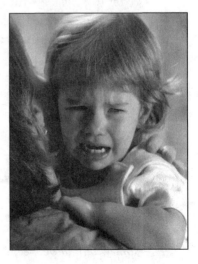

Intensity of Reaction: From Low Reactors to Big Reactors

Low Reactors are children who seem less demanding than others. Low Reactors tend to

- be quiet and rarely fuss;

- sleep more than average;

- show their emotions with only slight changes in facial expression, tone of voice, or body posture; and

- tolerate a lot of stimulation.

> **Parent Observations: At the Doctor's Office**
>
> *Gerry kicks her leg and protests with a soft whine when the doctor examines her.*
>
> *Reggie looks up at me, snuggles close as he can, and watches the doctor's every move with wide eyes.*
>
> *Tamisa screams and kicks her legs so hard that I think she might fly off my lap when the doctor listens to her heart.*

The fact that these children are less demanding, however, doesn't necessarily mean that they require less effort on the part of parents. On the contrary, you may have to work harder to attract and hold their attention.

At the other end of the spectrum are children like Carlos—Big Reactors—who tell the world how they feel in a voice that's loud and clear. Big Reactors tend to

- express their feelings with great intensity (for example, showing supreme happiness by squealing with delight and maybe expressing anger by shouting, throwing things, hitting, and biting); and

- react to physical stimuli every bit as intensely as they react to emotional stimuli (for example, perhaps being unable to tolerate irritants such as an itchy tag on a T-shirt, the wrinkle in a sock, or an unpleasant smell).

For many children, intensity isn't an issue at all. Their reactions fall somewhere between Low and Big Reactors, and they tend to take things in stride. Their moods are fairly even. They smile when they're happy and complain, in a reasonable way, when they're not.

*What do **you** think?*

> *How does my child react to sensory stimulation (sights, sounds, textures, smells, and tastes)?*

> *How much stimulation can my child handle? Does he react to the slightest bit of stimulation, does it take a lot to get him to respond, or are his reactions somewhere in between?*

> *Does my child express her feelings with high, moderate, or low intensity?*

> *How often do I find myself helping my child calm down?*

> *How much help does my child need to calm down?*

Your Child's Intensity of Reaction

As you reflect on your observations, how would you rate your child's intensity of reaction?

1 . . . . 2 . . . . 3 . . . . 4 5
Low Intensity   High Intensity

How You Might Respond When a Child Has a Low Reaction

- **Tune things up to attract her attention.** Watch your child's reactions to make sure she is engaged but not overexcited. Choose music with a dynamic beat. Engage your child in rough-and-tumble play. Use a dramatic voice while reading. Be silly and creative.

- **Create interactive games.** Devise activities that involve taking turns so your child remains engaged.

- **Get her body moving.** Low-intensity children may be more responsive if they're physically engaged.

- **Follow his lead.** If your child sings, join in for a duet. If he dances, become his partner.

How You Might Respond When a Child Has a Big Reaction

- **Tune things down.** Music and lighting should be soft. Clothing should be soft. And play should be fun, but not overstimulating.

- **Offer physical comfort when your child is distressed.** Hold her close, massage her back, rock her.

- **Show that you understand him by validating his feelings.** For example, use expressions such as "I know it's hard for you to be in crowded, noisy places" and "I know your feelings get so-o-o hurt."

- **Tell the story of what has just happened to help her feel in control.** For example, you might say, "You were angry that we had to leave, and you hit me to show me how angry you were."

- **Suggest and model alternative ways to respond.** For example, you might say, "It is not okay to hit. It hurts. You can hit this pillow instead."

- **Anticipate blowups.** Gently remove your child from potentially explosive situations. Try redirecting—getting him engaged in a different activity—or just give him a big hug.

- **As she grows, invite your child to help solve problems.** An example of how you might start this process is by saying, "You're going to a very noisy, crowded party today. What can we do to make it more comfortable for you?"

- **Don't punish your child for who she is.** Your child is not overreacting. Holding her close and validating her feelings can help your child calm down and feel safe and secure. Then, when she is old enough, help your child express those strong feelings in a more controlled way—through words or even by drawing those feelings.

Activity Level: From Sitters to Movers and Shakers

Some children are not action oriented. They are content to sit and play quietly. They tend to

- take the world in by looking or listening; and
- prefer exploring with their hands (using their fine motor skills) instead of their large muscles (arms and legs). They can often persist for long periods, working on a problem such as how to get the puzzle piece to fit or how to make the clown pop up.

Their interest in the things around them can be every bit as intense as the interest of an active baby, but they don't feel the same need to be up and about.

Other children are movers. They probably spent lots of time in mom's belly kicking and rolling around. They often develop into toddlers who are always on the go, exploring the world around them by crawling, running, and climbing. These movers and shakers

- love spaces that offer lots of opportunity for movement;
- are likely to keep moving until they drop; and
- like to reach out for and touch anything they can get their hands on.

Their activity level isn't an indication of a problem; it's just their preferred way of interacting and exploring. Their parents may be exhausted, but they definitely stay in shape!

Parent Observations:
Arriving at the Park

I hold out my arms and ask Sara if she's ready to get out of her stroller. She looks at me, smiles, and says, "Yes." When I put her down on the ground, she pauses and looks around, puts her hand in mine, and leads me to the sandbox.

Leo reaches up his arms to me and says, "Up!" I lift him out of his stroller. He heads straight to the slide.

José starts to climb out of the stroller as soon as he sees we are approaching the park. I reach down to be sure he doesn't fall. The moment his feet hit the ground, he is off and running—first to the slide, then over to the jungle gym, then into the sandbox where he grabs a shovel and starts digging.

Most kids fall somewhere in the middle. They enjoy running, climbing, and jumping, but they are also happy sitting with a puzzle or a book. They move easily from a quiet activity to a more active one.

What do you think?
➣ *What are my child's favorite activities? What makes him prefer these?*

➣ *Does my child prefer more action-oriented activities or quieter ones?*

➣ *How much of the day does my child spend in motion? How often do I find myself saying things like, "slow down," "take it easy," and "let's take a break"?*

➣ *How does my child respond when her movement is limited—when she is told, for example, not to crawl on the grocery store floor?*

➣ *How does my child explore a new place? A new activity?*

Your Child's Activity Level
As you reflect on your observations, how would you rate your child's activity level?

1 . . . . 2 . . . . 3 . . . . 4 5
Sitter   Mover and Shaker

How You Might Respond When a Child Is Less Active
- **Respect his pace and style.** Offer your child lots of opportunities to play with the things that he enjoys—for example, books, dress-up clothes, puzzles, building blocks, toy figures, etc. (And remember, you still need to baby-proof the house, even if he is not moving around a lot!)

- **Add movement to things she already enjoys.** Entice your child to move by holding a favorite toy a little beyond her easy reach or by starting to play with an interesting toy a little beyond where she can easily move.

continued

Your Child's Activity Level *continued*

- **Let your child look before he leaps.** If your child prefers watching kids on the climbing gym, let him watch. Then suggest trying something together—like going down the slide on your lap. But always remember to follow your child's lead, and take it slowly.

- **Play hide-and-seek.** When one of you is "found," entice your child into a chasing game.

- **Listen to music together.** It's easy to shift from listening to dancing if the music moves you!

- **Remember, there's nothing wrong with being a "sitter."** As long as your child gets the exercise he needs and can enjoy a range of activities he can be happy and healthy.

How You Might Respond to a Child Who Is a Mover and Shaker

- **Offer lots of opportunities for safe, active exploration.** Baby-proof your entire home. Create obstacle courses with pillows on the floor. Play hide-and-seek, freeze tag, and other active games.

- **Don't expect your child to lie or sit still for long.** Let her stand for a diaper change, give her permission to leave the high chair as soon as she is done eating, and allow her to turn the pages or act out the story when you read a book.

- **Engage your child's help with everyday activities.** Ask him to carry spoons to the table, help pick up leaves, and put all of the clean socks in a pile.

- **Recognize that your child will need extra time to wind down.** Start limiting active play at least an hour before bedtime and perhaps 30 minutes before naptime to help her slow down.

- **Remember, active children aren't wild or out of control.** They just need to move.

Persistence, Patience, and Frustration: From "I-Give-Up" Kids to "Let's-Try-Again" Kids

Persistence means not giving up when faced with a challenge. It is the ability to stick with a difficult task and cope with frustration. Children who are easily frustrated tend to get very upset the minute something doesn't go their way, have a hard time waiting for attention or help, and give up quickly when faced with a challenge. Children who are persistent usually keep trying when faced with a challenge, don't lose it when they don't get their way, and can tolerate waiting for their needs to be met.

What do you think?
- *How often does my child get frustrated?*
- *How does my child react when she is having a hard time doing something?*
- *What kinds of situations aggravate my child?*
- *Are there certain circumstances that my child finds most challenging (for example, during certain times of day, when he is tired)?*
- *What works in helping my child when she is frustrated? Will she accept help?*

Parent Observations: Building Block Towers

I hear Abby loudly grunting when the tower she is building tumbles. She starts building again, and when that one falls, she starts stamping her feet and screaming for me. When I come over, I suggest that maybe I could help her this time. She just screams, "No!" All I can do is hold her and wait until she quiets down.

When Kyle's block tower topples, he starts building again. After about three towers fall, he finds his car nearby on the rug and turns his tower into a road. He calls me to come see it. When I tell him I'll be right there, he calls me again. I come over, and he says, "Look Daddy. My road."

Karla builds a tower waist-high before it tumbles. She begins again. When it gets to her waist, it falls again. She rebuilds about five times. She tells me she wants to get it to be as tall as her. She won't give up, even though her plan is clearly not working. When I suggest another way to build the tower that may help her get it higher, she rejects my suggestion and continues doing it her way.

Your Child's Frustration Tolerance

As you reflect on your observations, how would you rate your child's way of dealing with frustration?

1 . . . . 2 . . . . 3 . . . . 4 5
I give up   I'll try again

How You Might Respond to a Child Who Will Not Give Up
- **If your child has to wait for something (food, attention, etc.), talk to him about what you are doing.** For example, you might say, "I'm taking your food out of the fridge" or "Daddy is taking his coat off and coming to give you a big hug."

continued

Your Child's Frustration Tolerance *continued*

- **When your child falls apart, let her know that you appreciate how hard it can be.** Think of using statements such as "Puzzles are hard! It makes you so mad when the bear won't fit in the space." Then become her coach. Rather than come to the rescue, help your child think through solutions without doing the work for her. Suggest or demonstrate strategies such as trying another space for the bear.

- **Teach your child to pace himself when frustration is building.** Offer time away from the frustrating task for a hug or a cozy snuggle with a book. Then return to the challenge with new energy. If a certain toy is creating a lot of frustration for your child, consider putting it away for a week or two and then trying again.

- **Maintain your sense of humor.** Children will appreciate it if, for example, you yell at the block that has fallen: "You silly block! You just won't stay up there! Well, you can't beat us; we're not giving up if it takes us all day!"

- **Model how to cope with frustration.** When you're struggling to fix something (or to put together your child's latest newfangled toy), try to remain calm. Say, "Wow, this is really hard!! I could use some help figuring this out. Would you like to help?" Or, put it away, showing your child that sometimes you just need to know when to take a break.

- **Try again later.** An activity that seems impossible when a child is hungry for lunch or has just recovered from a fall may be very manageable later. Try coming back to tasks when your child is well rested, fed, and in a positive mood.

- **Remember, although your child may never be the most patient and persistent person, you can do a lot to help your child learn to cope.**

How You Might Respond to a Persistent Child

- **Join your child in his play.** It's easy to let your child play alone for long periods because he is less demanding of your presence. But your child needs and benefits from your interaction together, and you can help him build new skills.

- **As your child grows, let her know that everyone needs help sometimes and that you are available.** Sometimes, children get so much positive feedback for being independent that it's hard for them to ask for help when they do need it.

- **Check to see whether your child is "spinning his wheels" by trying the same strategy over and over.** Sometimes, persistent kids can get stuck this way. If it happens, suggest new ways to approach the challenge.

- **Help your child to let go sometimes.** A persistent child may have a hard time accepting no for an answer. For example, even though you've said no more TV, your child keeps asking and asking. Be firm in your response and redirect her to something that she *is* allowed to do.

Reaction to New People: From "Let's-Take-It-Slow" Kids to "Glad-to-Meet-You" Kids

Some children are hesitant and shy around people they don't know. They tend to

- need time and support from trusted caregivers to warm up before they feel comfortable enough to interact;
- may be very happy to play on their own or with just one familiar friend or adult;
- are eager to hang out with you; and
- are likely to be just as content as more social and outgoing children.

Other children approach new people—adults and children—eagerly. They tend to

- engage newcomers by smiling, cooing, and looking them in the eye, even as babies; and
- project a sense of openness and ease, which elicits warm, positive responses from those they meet.

Most children fall somewhere in the middle. Sometimes they're hesitant and need some help and support around new people, and sometimes, they jump right in.

What do you think?
➤ *How does my child typically react when meeting someone new?*
➤ *Is my child more comfortable with adults, other children, or both?*
➤ *How does my child react when he is in a group situation?*
➤ *What kind of help, if any, does my child usually need from me when meeting new people and entering new situations?*

> **Parent Observations: In the Store Checkout Line**
> A woman in line behind us says, "Hello." Lisa looks at her for a moment, then reaches for me to pick her up out of the cart. When I do, Lisa buries her head in my shoulder, taking a peek now and then as the woman asks how old she is.
>
> ———
>
> Reggie looks at me, then at our fellow shopper. He looks at me again, then smiles at her and says, "Reggie" when she asks him his name.
>
> ———
>
> When the woman says, "Hello sweetie!" Henry smiles. When she looks away for a moment, he makes some noises and reaches out toward her to get her attention again.

Your Child's Approach to New People

As you reflect on your observations, how would you rate your child's approach to new people?

1 . . . . 2 . . . . 3 . . . . 4 5
Let's take it slow   I'm glad to meet you

How You Might Respond to a "Let's-Take-It-Slow" Child

- **Think of yourself as a safe home base.** Introduce your child to new people from the safety of your arms. Place her on your lap near another child and talk about what the other child is doing in a soothing, reassuring voice.

- **Communicate positive feelings toward others nonverbally.** Use your facial expressions and body language. Your child looks to you for cues.

- **Suggest that new people take it slow when they interact with your child.** Give them your child's favorite toy or book, and let them use it as a bridge to connect with him.

- **Whenever possible, prepare your child to meet new people ahead of time, and give her lots of time to get used to places such as a new child-care center before you leave him.** Share something about the new situation or person that will help your child know what to expect and that also might intrigue him—for example, "We're going to a new friend's house together. They have a dog." The more he knows ahead of time, the more comfortable your child will feel.

- **Use children's books and photographs to help your child know what to expect.** Books about meeting new people, going to a new school, or other encounters with "the unknown" can help your child have an idea of what to expect in a new situation. Showing your child pictures of the people she will be seeing can also help her to prepare and feel more familiar with them.

- **Don't label your child as "shy."** Labels can stick and become self-fulfilling prophecies. You can just explain to your child and to others that he likes to take things slow.

How You Might Respond to a "Glad-to-Meet-You" Child

- **Provide lots of opportunity for social interaction.** The glad-to-meet-you child thrives on it.

- **Be ready to step in when needed.** Even the most sociable child can find himself in situations where a helping hand is needed to resolve an argument or soothe hurt feelings. By stepping in when needed, you help ensure that time spent with peers is safe and enjoyable.

Your Child's Approach to New People *continued*

- **Watch for well-intended overenthusiasm.** If your child tends toward overexuberance, and perhaps knocks a child down with a big hug or even bites, help her express excitement in less physical ways. For example, make a game of taking turns hugging each other to help her learn what feels good and what is too rough.

- **Give your child time to play on his own.** Playing alone is a very different experience than playing with other children. Giving your child the chance to use his own resources and imagination helps him learn that he can be content not only with friends but also alone.

Coping With Change: From "I-Like-Things-the-Way-They-Are" Kids to "Show-Me-What's-New" Kids

Some children find changes hard. Even though young children—regardless of their capacity to cope with changes—are well known for being inflexible about their routines, some children seem to be even more dependent on them. And although few children like to stop an activity they were enjoying or haven't completed, some children have much more difficulty with transitions. These children tend to

- react to even the smallest of shifts—a new nipple on the bottle, a new food on their plate, or a slight change in a regular routine;

- thrive on order and predictable routines to feel safe and secure;

- have more tantrums, which can be triggered by anything from the suggestion of a new babysitter to a change of furniture in their house to the idea that they have to stop doing something they are happily immersed in; and

- need lots of time and support to get comfortable in new surroundings or with new people, generating lots of "No, No, No!" outbursts before they adjust.

> *Parent Observations:*
> *Visiting a Friend*
>
> Amanda resists even getting out of her car seat when she looks at the house we are parked in front of and doesn't recognize it. She clings to me for dear life when we enter the house and refuses to be put down the entire time we are there.
>
> Timothy hides behind me as we enter our friend's house. After a few minutes, he pulls me over to the toy shelf. Another child sits down next to him, and they soon begin to play together.
>
> Frederico runs up the path, bangs on the door, and runs straight into the playroom as soon as our friend opens the door.

Other children take change in stride. They tend to

- find new jackets, new friends, new foods, and new babysitters interesting; and

- respond comfortably anywhere you take them because they nap in noisy restaurants, nurse wherever you happen to be, and, when older, enjoy looking around, drawing on the paper you tucked in your bag, or joining in the conversation.

Most children fall somewhere in the middle. They may have an easy time with new foods, but a more difficult time with new places. They may be cautious around unknown adults, but perfectly comfortable with new peers. Given some time to get used to a change or new situation, they feel safe, at ease, and eager to explore.

What do you think?

➤ *How does my child react to a change in routine?*

➤ *How does my child react to a new place or situation?*

➤ *How easy is it for me to shift my child from one activity to the next—bath to bed, park to home, play to dinner?*

➤ *Does my child enjoy trying new things and eating new foods, or does she prefer to stick with what's familiar?*

➤ *What kind of help, if any, does my child usually need from me to handle change?*

Your Child's Response to Change

As you reflect on your observations, how would you rate your child's response to change?

1 . . . . 2 . . . . 3 . . . . 4 5
I like things the way they are   I'm up for anything

How You Might Respond When a Child Shows That He Prefers Things the Way They Are

- **Use familiar objects to ease anxiety during transitions.** A new doctor will be less scary if your child has her favorite blanket or stuffed animal in hand.

- **Let your child be part of the transition.** Give your child a sense of control over what is going on by putting napkins on the table when it is time to get ready for dinner, or pressing the button to turn off the TV.

- **Ease into new activities.** Talk about new activities first, and arrive early enough to allow your child to get comfortable.

- **Offer advance notice when an activity is about to end.** For example, you might say, "When this book is finished, we're going home" or "When the timer rings, it's time for your bath."

Your Child's Response to Change *continued*

- **Show appreciation and encouragement when she has made a transition.** For example, you could say, "You got into the car seat so quickly. That's great!" This kind of reinforcement may make future transitions easier.

- **Offer realistic choices as he gets older.** Give your child a sense of control about how he wants to make transitions. For example, you might say, "Would you like to sing one more song before we leave?"

How You Might Respond When a Child Shows That She Is Eager to Try Something New

- **Be sensitive to your child's signals.** When a child is extremely easygoing, it is easy to take for granted that any change is okay.

- **Let your child know about new situations ahead of time.** For example, tell him before going to a new place or meeting someone new. Children who enjoy new situations also enjoy talking about and anticipating them.

- **Be sure to find some one-on-one quiet time to enjoy together.** No matter how easily a child can handle being out in the world, there's nothing like taking time to snuggle on the living room couch and look at a favorite book together.

Remember—

- *Parenting is like being a detective. Watching what your child does on the "outside" gives you important clues about what is happening on the inside.*

- *Understanding your child's behavior involves putting together clues of context, developmental age and stage, and temperament—as you would do with pieces of a puzzle.*

CHAPTER 3

Step 3: Make Sensitive and Effective Decisions

SENSITIVE AND EFFECTIVE DECISION MAKING means using what you know about yourself and what you have learned by tuning in to your child to find a good "fit" and handle everyday parenting challenges.

Finding Your Fit

You and your child each have your own way of approaching the world, your own interests and preferences. (And, needless to say, you are at very different stages of your development!) Whether you and your child are very alike or very different, seeing and appreciating how you "fit"—and don't "fit"—together will help you make decisions that nurture your child's well-being and talents.

There's No Such Thing as a Perfect Fit

Parenting is like dancing. You take a "step" and your child responds. She takes a step and you respond. Sometimes you take the lead, sometimes he does. But no parent and child—in fact, hardly any two people—can dance together for very long without a misstep or two.

The goal is not to change the other person, but to watch their "moves" and adapt. For example, a parent who likes to be active doesn't force his child, who prefers to use his hands and create through art, to play sports. A parent who needs quiet time for himself but has a highly active child helps his child learn to slow down sometimes. Adapting to each other's rhythms and interests allows you to learn from each other and create a special dance that works for both of you much of the time.

Being temperamentally similar to your child comes with its own challenges. For example, when parent and child are both intense, a parent may have a harder time calming her child because she is so worked up herself. A slow-to-warm-up dad may have a hard time helping his shy child enter a new situation because of his own discomfort.

Whether you and your child are similar or different, you can't dance for very long without learning a step or two from the other. Adapting to one another's rhythm offers opportunities to learn from the other's strengths and interests. It also helps your child learn about how to get along with others who are not exactly like her—a skill that will serve her well in the future.

How You and Your Child Are Alike and Different

We invite you to use the tool below to compare how you and your child are temperamentally alike and different. It may also be useful to have other adults in your child's life use it. You can then compare notes to learn how different adults see your child, how their fit may be different from yours, and what the differences may mean for your child.

Comparing Temperaments

For each trait below, draw a circle to show where you see your child on the continuum. Then mark an X to show where you see yourself. (Note: To include other adults, use a different symbol for each adult.)

Intensity of reaction:

1 . . . . 2 . . . . 3 . . . . 4 5
Even tempered/laid back   Intense reactor

Reaction to new people:

1 . . . . 2 . . . . 3 . . . . 4 5
Loves meeting new people   Very anxious meeting new people

Response to change:

1 . . . . 2 . . . . 3 . . . . 4 5
Makes changes easily   Very upset by change

Activity level:

1 . . . . 2 . . . . 3 . . . . 4 5
Mover and shaker   Sitter

Frustration tolerance:

1 . . . . 2 . . . . 3 . . . . 4 5
Never gives up   Very easily frustrated

What do **you** *think?*
> *How are you and your child alike? What effect do these similarities have on your relationship?*
> *How are you and your child different? What effect do these differences have on your relationship?*

Adapting to Your Child's Style

Regardless of your similarities and differences, your child needs you to understand and adapt to his style as much you can. He needs you to alter your rhythm and steps, if necessary, without denying your own feelings and needs, so your dance together is in sync as much as possible. Keep in mind that as you adjust to him, he is adapting to you—to the way you hold him, feed him, and talk to him. Appreciating and enjoying your child for who he is will make him feel valued and secure, feelings that help him develop a strong, positive sense of self. But sometimes this is easier said than done.

Depending on your own temperament, some of your child's characteristics will be easier to adapt to than others. For example, if you express your emotions with great passion, you may feel that something is missing if your child shows her excitement with just a small grin. If you are a persistent person, yet your child has a low threshold for frustration, engaging in some activities together may be challenging.

Remember Frank and Carlos, the toddlers that we met in Chapter 2? Let's look at how their parents adapt to their individual style.

When Sasha gets upset, she explodes. She screeches and tries to kick and hit me. Sometimes I just lose it myself, shout at her, and sometimes squeeze her wrists too roughly as I try to talk some sense into her. When we're out in public and this kind of thing happens, I feel really embarrassed—like people are thinking I'm a terrible mother. Now I see that at least part of the problem is that we are both really intense and that I need to learn to have better control because she needs me to help her calm down.

Rachel seems so different from me. She always wants to be moving. I'd rather sit and read a good book. The good news is she's gotten me into much better shape and I'm doing things I haven't done in a long time—like playing ball and running. We now take little jogs together around the block.

Spencer hates change. I have to give him advance warning about everything, which does not come naturally to me because I, unfortunately, am not a planner at all.

Frank—the toddler who is slow and cautious about entering new situations—can be a challenge for his mom, Sara. Even though she sees herself as a slow-to-warm-up person too, life would be easier if Frank took to change more easily. But Frank's cautious approach to the world is a major challenge for Robert, Frank's dad, who is a jump-right-in kind of guy. He finds it easier to be with Frank's older sister, Alicia, whose style is more like his. Three weeks ago, when Sara was in bed with the flu, Robert decided to spend the afternoon in the park with

Frank. To his surprise and dismay, he realized it had been a long time since they had done something together, in part because of his discomfort with Frank's cautious personality.

Robert and Sara talk and come up with some ideas to help Frank feel more comfortable in new situations. They agree to try these ideas out for a few weeks, then evaluate how things are going and decide whether they should try anything new or different. They plan to try the following strategies:

> ### Strategies to Help You Find Your Fit
> - **Be aware of and think about your reactions to your child's behavior.** *What is it about this behavior that makes me react so strongly, so negatively, or both? Does it remind me of something about myself or someone else (parent, brother, sister, uncle, aunt) whom I do or don't particularly like? How does it make me feel about myself as a parent?*
>
> - **Avoid making comparisons between your child and others and between yourself and other parents.** *No two children, parents, or families are alike, so comparisons are often useless. (Next time you see a parent and child and think, "That mom has it so easy," ask her about it. You may be surprised.)*
>
> - **Talk with other adults who know your child.** *How you see your child may be very different from how your spouse, partner, or other caregivers see her. For example, Ruby, the mom of Alice—a feisty toddler—thought that other parents didn't like Alice because she was so "mouthy." Then one day, one of the moms in their playgroup commented on how self-assured Alice was and how she wished that her own daughter was more confident, like Alice.*

- Choose new experiences that they think Frank will enjoy once he adjusts to them—for example, riding on the train at the zoo.

- Help Frank feel more comfortable by talking in advance about where they will be going and what it might be like; they decide to read books with him about zoos and trains.

- Let Frank make choices, like deciding what to do at the zoo and how long they will stay.

Carlos—the intense and strong-willed toddler who lives with his grandmother, Louise—often overwhelms her. He has trouble controlling his strong emotions. At first, Louise saw Carlos's big reactions as being "bad," and she would punish him. But after talking with his preschool teacher, she has come to understand that Carlos's intense reactions are part of his nature. She decides to help Carlos develop better self-control by trying the following strategies:

- Give Carlos lots of advance notice about what is going to happen next, which makes him feel more in control and less easily upset.

- Stay calm in the face of Carlos's intensity, which is relatively easy for Louise to do because of her even-tempered nature.

- Identify early warning signs of potential upset and offer help when she sees frustration mounting.

- Label his feelings and let him know that he is not alone, which will help Carlos feel more in control of his emotions and better able to cope. It will also let him know that he is safe and can trust his grandmother to understand and support him.

What do you think?
➤ *Think of a time when you adapted to your child's behavior and helped her to cope. What did you do? What was the outcome?*
➤ *What might you decide to do the same or differently next time?*

Making Everyday Decisions

To illustrate how you can put together what you know about yourself and your child to make sensitive and effective decisions, we have chosen to focus on sleep and discipline—two of the most challenging issues that parents face. The three-step approach to decision making that is described here can be applied to almost any parenting challenge that you face and will help you make the best decisions possible.

As you read the following vignettes, you may begin to wonder, like the father in Chapter 1, whether you will have to quit your job to have time to go through these steps. Needless to say, the realities of everyday life mean you often won't have the time or energy to think about every situation with your child in this in-depth way. The good news is you don't need to. Over time, this approach will become a part of your thinking process. Many parents have told us that, even if they don't methodically go through each step, just being aware of the steps helps them be less reactive and make better decisions. They find themselves stopping and thinking more, which helps them respond to their child in a way that they feel is more effective. We start with sleep.

Sleep
For many parents, sleep is one of the toughest issues they face. Whether the challenge involves getting into bed to begin with, falling asleep, or waking in the middle of the night, the process of using what you know about yourself and carefully observing what's going on with your child can help you address the problem. Here's one family's experience with using the three-step approach to decision making.

Renee, mother of strong, healthy, 9-month-old Jason, is very unhappy about the fact that Jason is still waking up twice a night for feedings. She hoped and expected that he would be sleeping through the night by now. She is becoming very irritable.

Renee had a difficult pregnancy after several miscarriages. Jason has been a very demanding and intense baby. Renee had planned on staying home with Jason for the first year, but she had to go back to work and put Jason in child care when he was 6 months old because her husband lost his job.

Renee discusses with her pediatrician the need to get Jason to sleep through the night. He suggests that, when Jason wakes up in the middle of the night, Renee should try a plan that is popular with many parents: going in every few minutes to comfort him until he falls asleep again. Renee tries this plan for several consecutive nights, but Jason just protests harder and harder every time Renee walks out of the room. Renee finally "gives in" and nurses him back to sleep.

Step 1: Use what you know about yourself.

Renee examines her reaction to the situation and identifies the following important factors that are affecting her thoughts and actions: "I love Jason so much. I find I worry about him a lot. I can't stand to hear him fuss or protest. I'm afraid he will feel abandoned if I don't comfort him right away when he cries at night, especially since I now have to leave him in child care. At the same time, I'm exhausted and feeling tired and annoyed all the time."

2 Step 2: Use what you know about your child.

Next, Renee thinks about what Jason brings to the situation.

- **What's happening in my child's world?** "Maybe Jason is picking up on my stress and tension. Maybe that makes it harder for him to relax and separate from me at bedtime. Also, I often nurse Jason to sleep even though my pediatrician told me that kids who don't fall asleep on their own wake up a lot more in the middle of the night. It's a really nice way of feeling close to him, especially now that we're apart during the day."

- **Where is my child developmentally?** "Jason now knows that things still exist even though he can't see them. So, now, when I walk out of the room, Jason knows I'm still out there somewhere, which is why he may be crying—to make me come back."

• **What is my child's temperament?** "Jason is very 'emotional.' When he is happy, he is elated, and when he is mad, he is in a rage. There is no in-between. He also doesn't like change. He needs things to be predictable. I have to move slowly and give him lots of time to adjust to anything new. So I'm sure the transition to child care and the tension at home are affecting him."

Renee also notices that Jason is very sensitive when it comes to noise. He startles when there is a sudden, loud sound, and he even reacts when music changes in intensity.

3 Step 3: Practice sensitive and effective decision making.

Renee comes up with some ideas to try to help Jason sleep through the night. Her ideas may be similar to or different from what you would come up with in the same situation. Remember, there is no right and wrong here. What's important is to use what you know to respond in the way that you think will work best for your child—and then to make corrections if it doesn't work out as you had hoped and expected. (Remember, trial and error leads to trial and success.)

Helping Jason Sleep Through the Night

What Renee knows	What Renee is going to try
Jason is very reactive to noise.	Put a white-noise machine in his room or let soft music play in his room to drown out noises in the house.
I want Jason to learn to fall asleep on his own.	I won't let him fall asleep while nursing.
I need to let Jason fuss a little. Jason needs reassurance that I am still there now that he understands "object permanence." Jason needs predictability.	If he protests when I lay him down in his crib, I'll go to him once to gently pat him and let him know that I am still there and that everything's okay. I won't keep coming in and out. That only confuses him.
I need help to resist going to "rescue" him when I hear him crying.	I will remind myself that I love him and am trying to do what is best for him—and that a good night's sleep will give me more energy and make me feel more loving toward Jason. I will try to distract myself with a book or the TV until he settles down.
I need more help from Joe (Jason's dad).	I will talk with Joe about the possibility of him putting Jason to bed at night. That will take some of the stress off me, and maybe Jason will have a different response to him.

Discipline

As in all other aspects of child rearing, there is no one-size-fits-all approach to discipline. So many factors go into deciding what limits to set and how to set them: the context for the behavior, your child's stage of development, and your child's temperament. In addition, your own beliefs, values, and expectations for how you want your child to behave play important roles. (This complexity is the key reason why we offer a process, or framework, for solving parenting challenges, not specific prescriptions. Most parents of more than one child will tell you that, even within the same family, what works for one child doesn't work for the other.) Let's look at how the decision-making process might work for a family with two very different children who require different approaches to discipline.

> *Stacy and Ed, who both work outside the home, have two children, Robbie, 19 months, and Kyla, 3 years. Robbie is into everything. He never seems to stop moving, and he is very strong willed. He wants to do everything by himself and throws tantrums when he is thwarted. He wants to feed himself, pour his own milk, and walk the dog. He shouts, hits, and throws things when he is frustrated that he can't do it "by myself!"*

> *Kyla is more passive and slow to warm up. When things don't go her way, she doesn't protest openly but, instead, pulls away and protests quietly. Recently, while Kyla was happily playing in the sandbox, her dad told her it was time to leave the park. She protested by walking all the way home at a snail's pace. And she would not respond when mom or dad tried to engage her.*

> *Stacy is at her wit's end with Robbie, with whom she finds herself in constant power struggles. She has removed him from situations, taken away special toys and TV time, and put him in time-outs. Nothing seems to get him to cooperate. Ed doesn't have nearly as many power struggles with Robbie.*

> *On the other hand, Ed and Stacy do very little disciplining of Kyla. She seems so fragile and gets very upset when anger is expressed, especially toward her. When she does misbehave, which is rare, they tend to let it go.*

Step 1: Use what you know about yourself.

When Stacy and Ed ask themselves what they bring to the situation, Stacy identifies the following factors: "I like to feel in control. To make things worse, I'm a clean freak and hate when things are messy and disorganized. Robbie makes me anxious because I never know what he is going to get into next or when the next blowup will be. I find Kyla much easier to deal with. She's so easy."

Ed identifies these factors. "I'm more laid back, more easygoing than Stacy. I like, and actually admire, Robbie's spunk and how assertive and independent he is. I worry about Kyla. She gives up too easily. She's not a fighter."

Step 2: Use what you know about your child.

As Stacy and Ed tune in to what their children bring to the situation, they ask:

- **What's going on in the kids' world?** "With both of us working, we don't have the time we'd like with Robbie and Kyla. And Stacy's dad is ill. Caring for him is taking a lot of our financial resources and energy. By the end of the day, we are both too tired to think. We are in 'react' mode. We lose it with Robbie and pay too little attention to Kyla."

- **Where are the children developmentally?** "We know Robbie is at an age when kids want to be more independent—and he can be independent because he can now run, climb, talk, and especially figure out how to get what he wants! At the same time, we understand that he can't yet stop himself from doing something we have told him countless times is a no-no. Kyla can have real conversations with us now and can tell us what she is thinking. She also loves to play pretend."

- **What are the children's individual approaches to being in the world—their temperaments?** "Robbie is no doubt a high-intensity, very active, persistent kid. He seems to crave physical contact. He loves to use his body any way he can. Kyla is a slow-to-warm up, quiet, low-intensity kid who tends to feel more comfortable playing alone or one-on-one. She really closes down in situations when too much is going on around her—like situations in which there is lots of noise and action. She'll just stay close to us, like she wants to be protected. She also gets very upset when she thinks she has made us angry."

Step 3: Practice sensitive and effective decision making.

Finally, Stacy and Ed come up with some ideas for setting limits.

Setting Limits for Robbie and Kyla

What Ed and Stacy know	What Ed and Stacy are going to try
We need to reduce our stress and have more energy for the kids.	Hire the 12-year-old neighbor to help out with household chores in the evenings and sometimes on weekends to free us up to focus more on the kids.
The power struggles are not good for Robbie (or Mom).	For now, Ed will be the chief limit setter to give Mom and Robbie a break and to give Dad more responsibility for discipline.
We need to find positive ways for Robbie to redirect his energy.	Think of safe, acceptable ways that Robbie can do his exploration: • Let him pour his own milk, but have him do it over the sink to reduce mess. • Give him lots of containers and toys to experiment with in the bathtub. • Let him walk the dog, but only if one of us is holding the leash with him.
Robbie needs more help to gain control.	Stacy will work on staying calm when Robbie is losing it. Label Robbie's feelings—for example, "It makes you so-o-o-o angry when you can't get your shoe on!" Give Robbie choices, within reasonable limits.
Robbie needs lots of opportunity for physical activity.	Be sure he has some time to play outside each day. Find ways he can play safely but actively in the house.
Kyla needs to feel more comfortable expressing her feelings and letting her needs be known.	Observe Kyla more carefully to figure out what she might be feeling. Give her words for her feelings and permission to express them.
Kyla needs limit setting, too.	Tell her when we don't like something she has done, gently but clearly. Help her handle "difficult" feelings.
We can help Kyla deal with and express her feelings through pretend play.	Join in her play. Make up stories and characters that give her practice managing difficult feelings and speaking up for herself.
Kyla needs more attention	Make sure Kyla doesn't get "lost" when we are overwhelmed by Robbie. Create special times when we each can have "alone time" with Kyla so that she can have some undivided attention.

Other Ways to Use the Three Steps

This three-step process can be useful in helping you make many other parenting decisions. Consider the following examples.

Planning Ahead for Future Child-Rearing Decisions

If you are thinking about starting to teach your child to use the potty, you might want to take the time to think about what your own hopes, expectations, and feelings are about it. Here's how one mom, Marta, applies the three steps to prepare for the upcoming potty training of her 29-month-old son, Luis.

┃ Step 1: Use what you know about yourself.

Marta is dreading potty training Luis because of all the horror stories she has heard from other parents. She is very concerned that the experience will be fraught with power struggles and frustration. With this awareness, she decides to think more positively and see if she can help create a different experience for Luis (and herself!).

2 Step 2: Use what you know about your child.

Marta knows that Luis is a very strong-willed child who does not like to be told what to do. He does much better when he feels that he has choices and is in control.

3 Step 3: Practice sensitive and effective decision making.

Marta decides that the best approach for Luis would be to provide tools (underwear, potty, etc.) and encouragement. She also thinks that reading books with him about learning to use the potty will help him feel more in control. What she will try very hard not to do is to get into power struggles with him. It will have to be his choice, even if it takes him a long time to learn.

Of course, each situation varies. Tamisa, another mom, uses the three-step approach in a different way to plan for toilet training.

┃ Step 1: Use what you know about yourself.

Tamisa wants her son, Derrick, to be trained before he turns 3. All her nieces and nephews were trained by that age, and she does not want her son to be an exception. She is also eager to save all the money she is currently spending on diapers!

2 **Step 2: Use what you know about your child.**

Tamisa knows that Derrick does not do well with change, and they have recently moved to a new neighborhood and a new child-care provider. So Tamisa recognizes that it will be important to give Derrick lots of time to make this big transition.

3 **Step 3: Practice sensitive and effective decision making.**

Tamisa plans to start preparing Derrick for toilet training between 18 months and 2 years of age—getting a kid-size potty, having him wear under-wear, and giving him rewards for using the potty.

Learning From What Works

Understanding why things go well can help you figure out what you can do to set the stage for more positive interactions. Think about an enjoy-able time that you've had with your child. Try to figure out what happened during that morning when dressing became a shared, creative en-deavor, or how the trip to the grocery store turned into a fun way to learn about colors and counting.

> *What do you think?*
> ➤ *What made this experience so enjoyable for you? (Self-awareness)*
> ➤ *What made this experience so enjoyable for your child? How do you know? (Tuning in to your child)*
> ➤ *What were the factors that you think made this experience a positive one? How can you re-create these circumstances more often? (Sensitive and effective decision making)*

Learning From What Doesn't Work

As we discussed earlier, "mistakes" can be great learning opportunities. Here's how one dad uses the three steps to make a course correction that helps him comfort his son.

Coping When Nothing Works
Roderick, a new dad, picks up his crying 3-week-old, Brandon and begins to rock him gently. But the more Roderick rocks, the more upset Brandon seems to become. Roderick tries everything he can think of—walking, holding him in different positions, swaddling him, putting him down to see whether he wants a break, even checking his temperature. But Brandon just keeps on crying.

Keep in mind that you are doing something very important for your child by not giving up. You are letting him know that he can trust you to be there for him, no matter what; that you may not have all the answers, but you will always love him and keep him safe. You may not be able to figure out why he's having a tantrum at that moment or even why he is having a difficult, cranky day. Maybe all you can do is hold him tight and let him know that you see what a hard time he's having. Simply being there for him, letting him know that he is not alone, is what matters.

James, a new dad, picks up his crying 3-week-old, Danny, and begins to rock him gently, as most parents would do. But the more James rocks, the more upset Danny seems to become. The more Danny cries, the more tense James feels. He feels so inadequate. He can't even calm his own son!

James takes a deep breath to calm himself. (Self-awareness) Now he can think about what other methods might work. He tries different strategies—walking Danny around the room, holding him in different positions, singing to him. Through his experimentation, James discovers that Danny doesn't like a lot of movement when he's upset. (Tuning in to his child) Instead, James decides to swaddle Danny in a blanket; he holds his son and feels him relax. (Sensitive and effective decision making)

In the past three chapters, we have focused on how your decisions can support your child. Now we look at how you can make decisions about promoting your child's healthy development with the other adults who help care for her.

Remember—
- *No matter what your similarities and differences are, your child needs you to try your best to understand and adapt to her style.*
- *Appreciating and enjoying your child for who he is will make him feel valued and secure, feelings that help him develop a strong, positive sense of self.*
- *Avoid making comparisons between your child and others and between yourself and other parents.*
- *The three-step approach can be applied to almost any parenting challenge you face, and it will help you make the best decision you can.*
- *Over time, this approach will become a natural part of your thinking process.*

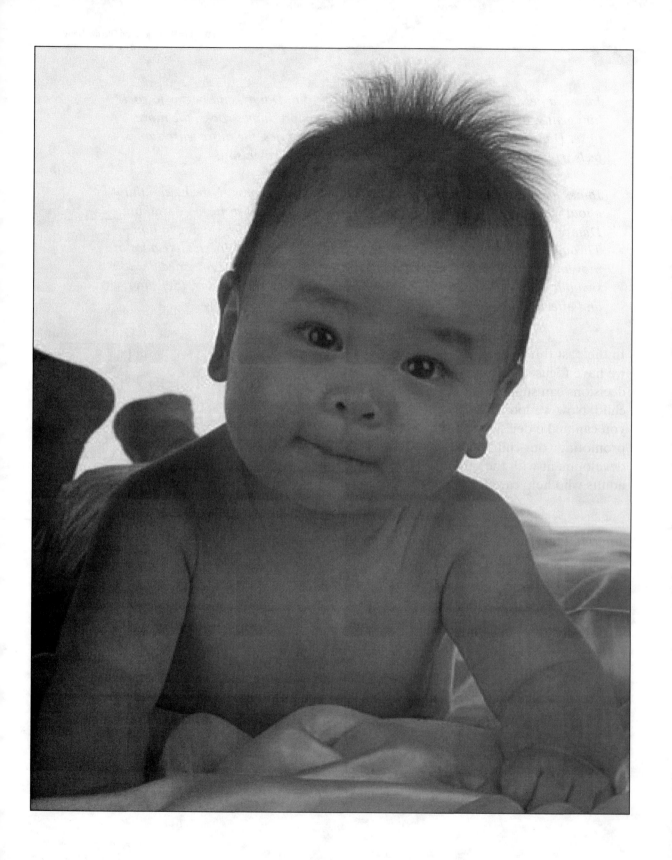

CHAPTER 4

Sharing the Care: Making Decisions With the Other Adults in Your Child's Life

SHARING THE CARE OF BABIES AND TODDLERS is a reality for most parents today. Whether you work in or outside the home, chances are you are sharing the care—to varying degrees—with a spouse, partner, other family members; people outside your family; or friends. Learning to work and make decisions together with the other trusted adults in your child's life is critical to your child's healthy development and your own sanity. Having more than one caregiver gives your child an opportunity to learn new things about himself and about others that can broaden and enrich his life. It can also give you a needed break. As one parent puts it, "I know I can't give my child everything she needs. The way I see it, other adults in her life fill in the gaps."

Another real benefit of sharing the care—as a story earlier in the book illustrated—is seeing your child through another person's eyes. For example, a dad who felt that his 2-year-old son, Bruce, was an untamable "Wild Man" was surprised and delighted when his child-care provider commented on what a leader Bruce was—that he was always thinking up great pretend dramas that all the kids wanted to take part in.

Yet sharing the care isn't always easy. Different people have different parenting styles, based on their cultural beliefs and values as well as their childhood experiences. Letting go and temporarily putting your child's care in another person's hands can be difficult—even if the other person is your spouse or partner.

Sharing the Care Evokes Strong Feelings

No matter how much you love your spouse or trust and respect your child's care provider, sharing the care of a young child can stir up strong feelings. The relief that you experience knowing that your child is in good hands as you go off to work or school, see a movie with your spouse, or have a cup of coffee with a friend is easy to handle. So, too, is the pleasure in knowing that your child is going to have the chance to finger paint or go to the park to dig for worms—especially if these activities top your "to be avoided" list.

But many parents also experience uncomfortable, hard-to-deal-with feelings such as jealousy, competition, and guilt.

> *Sheri, who just started back to work, is worried that her son will come to love his family child-care provider more than her. She finds herself avoiding interaction with the caregiver and doesn't talk about her at all with her son.*

> *Rachita storms out of the house, feeling angry and incompetent. After struggling to get her 3-year-old son, Alex, dressed for child care, he eagerly puts on his coat for his dad, Michael. Rachita is so upset she doesn't even pause to hug Michael and Alex good-bye and doesn't remind Alex, who likes to know what to expect, that she will pick him up at the end of the day. Although she later leaves a message at Alex's child-care program asking a caregiver to tell Alex that she will pick him up, she feels very guilty for the rest of the day about the way she left the house this morning.*

> *Ken stops by his mother's house to pick up his 2-year-old daughter, Allie. When he tells Allie it is time to go home, she announces, "No! I want to stay at Grandma's." Ken feels very hurt and wonders what he is doing wrong as a parent to get that reaction. He also feels jealous of and angry at his mother.*

Many of the parents and caregivers we have spoken with have shared similar feelings and experiences. These feelings are natural. Parents and caregivers develop fierce attachments to the infants and toddlers they care for, so the relationships that those children have with other adults can feel threatening. Putting these feelings on the table is very important because they can get in the way of adults working together in a child's best interests. The strategies and tools in the following pages can help you share the care with the other adults in your child's life in ways that support her development.

No One Can Take Your Place
Before continuing, let's lay to rest one of the biggest fears we hear from parents when it comes to sharing the care: Will my child love someone else more than me? The answer: No! No one can take your place. You are special to your child in ways that no one can replace.

Unfortunately, parents often find themselves questioning their supreme status in their child's life when, for example, they arrive at the child-care provider's house at the end of the day to find their child refusing to look at them or clinging to the caregiver while communicating through their actions or words, "I want to stay here!" This experience can be heartbreaking. But it doesn't mean your child loves her care-giver more than you. When you look at the sit-uation through your child's eyes, you will see that she is really saying, "I'm having such a good time here. I need a little time to adjust to the idea that it's time to go, and I also need some help to say good-bye." Or, "I missed you so much when you left. Then Ms. Lucy helped me have a good day. Suddenly, here you are. I need a little time to let go of Ms. Lucy and get used to being with you again." Through these hard-to-take declarations of love, your child is letting you know that she can trust you with her strongest feelings.

Fear of being replaced occurs at home, too. At various times during their child's early years, many parents complain to us that their child prefers the other parent. This behavior may be attributed to a developmental phase. It can also occur when one parent is spending significantly more time than the other in daily caregiving routines such as diapering, feeding, bathing, and comforting. It can also happen when one parent has an easier, more comfortable fit with a child than the other.

Sharing-the-care situations can trigger strong feelings such as pride, guilt, and jealousy. One dad told us, "It might sound terrible, but it made me feel good when our daughter insisted on being with me—even though I knew this was upsetting to my wife."

> ### Sharing the Care With Your Spouse: Alicia's Story
>
> When I hear our 2-year-old Thomas's frustration rising, I go into the living room to see what's going on. My husband, Ross, has just given him a new puzzle. It looks too hard for Thomas, so I go over to help him find the space for the bear piece he is holding in his hand. Ross motions me away. He begins to coach Thomas. "You're right; the bear definitely doesn't fit there. How about another space?" he asks, pointing to open spaces on the board. Thomas tries another space, but that doesn't work either. He's getting more frustrated and so am I. I think Ross is being too hard on Thomas, but Ross keeps on going. "Boy, this new puzzle is hard! It's going to take a lot of work! What about trying another space?" I give Ross some very dirty looks and start to approach Thomas to finally rescue him. But just before I act, to my surprise, Thomas finds the right space. He smiles with joy at his accomplishment.
>
> It took a lot of self-control for Alicia not to step in. Luckily, holding back allowed her an opportunity to see what would happen. She trusted her husband's good intentions enough to control her urges to rescue Thomas. She also had to accept that there is not one right way to parent a child and that her way is not the only way.

Two-year-old Sophie is cared for by her dad, Barry, while her mom, Katherine, works. At night, Katherine, who is eager to connect with Sophie, wants to read her a book before bed. Sophie refuses, insisting, "Only Daddy read!" Naturally, this rejection is very painful for Katherine. She also finds herself feeling annoyed with Dad, the "chosen" one. Katherine ends up just leaving the room.

To try to address and resolve their situation, Barry and Katherine use the three-step decision-making process. First, they work on step 1, being aware of and sharing one's feelings. Barry admits feeling badly for Katherine and guilty that he is the favored one. He also wants Sophie to accept Katherine so he can get a break at night. Katherine recognizes that her hurt feelings make her react defensively, rather than staying engaged.

Next, they consider step 2, tuning in to their child. They look at what's going on through Sophie's eyes to try to understand what she is feeling and thinking. Both Barry and Katherine recognize that Sophie needs to count on both of them to care for and love her. They also agree that, because Sophie spends so much time with Barry, it is probably more difficult for her to make the transition to being with Katherine when she gets home from work. Sophie does not like change. She relies heavily on routines and predictability to feel safe. Katherine sees that Sophie is not rejecting her; she simply wants to stay with the more familiar parent.

Finally, Barry and Katherine take step 3, using what they know to make a decision that supports their child. Barry and Katherine agree that they need to work together. They decide that Sophie should have more time alone with Mom on evenings and weekends. If Sophie protests, they will not give in, knowing that more time with Mom will mean less protesting in the future and better relationships all around. When

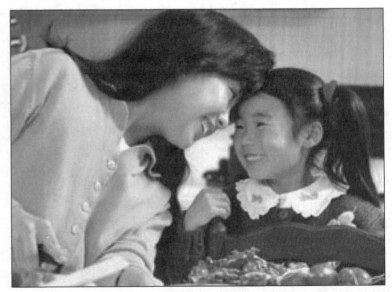

they are involved in an activity all together and Sophie protests, Barry explains, "I want Mommy here with us. She would like to take a turn reading to you, too." When Sophie still insists that only Barry read, he invites Katherine to sit close and to begin chiming in, sending Sophie the message that Mom belongs there, too. For her part, Katherine resists her impulse to just walk out. It helps to keep telling herself (a) that Sophie's behavior doesn't mean that Sophie doesn't love her, and (b) that walking away will only keep the cycle going. She knows she needs to hang in there to let Sophie know that she can count on both her parents to provide love, care, and security.

Saying Hello and Good-bye

Whether you are leaving your child with your spouse or a friend while you run to the supermarket or whether you are saying good-bye at child care and heading for work, the following suggestions can make hellos and good-byes easier for everyone:

- **Help your child prepare for separations.** *Play peek-a-boo and other disappearing– reappearing games with infants and toddlers. Read books about separations and reunions with 2- and 3-year-olds. If your child is going outside the home for care, make sure to visit the place several times before actually starting the care. If someone is caring for your child at your home, have the caregiver visit a few times when you are still at home so your child can begin to get to know the caregiver in the safety of your presence.*

- **Create rituals.** *Before you leave, start telling your young child a story or start drawing a picture together that you can finish when you return. Have a special saying at departure time such as "See you later alligator!" Give him a special kiss that's only meant for good-byes—like one on his nose or forehead.*

- **Work with your child-care provider to ease the separation.** *A provider can help get your child started on an activity before you leave. She can ask your child to be a special helper—like setting up breakfast or taking out the toys for that morning. The child-care provider can hold and comfort your child and, perhaps, take your child to the window to wave good-bye.*

- **Say good-bye. Avoid the temptation to sneak out.** *When you sneak out, you are sending your child the message that you are doing something wrong by leaving, which only increases her anxiety about the separation. It can also have a negative effect on her trust in you. Saying good-bye lets your child know that she can count on you to let her know what's going on. Saying good-bye tells your child that you respect and appreciate her feelings. It also means that your child doesn't have to wonder about or worry whether you are going to disappear again.*

Comparing Notes: A Tool for Making Decisions With the Other Adults in Your Child's Life

Communicating is key to making any partnership work. But busy schedules and feelings about sharing the care often interfere with parents' ability to discuss important information about their child's care with their caregivers.

We have included a tool on the next page to help you and your child's other caregivers (including your own spouse or partner) use the three-step approach to make decisions together in a way that supports your child's development and well-being. Each of you should think about or jot down your answers to the questions in parts one and two. Then, find a time when you can sit down together—ideally, without interruption—to share your responses. Use the information and ideas that emerge in this discussion to answer the questions in part three together. Try to do this exercise every few months or whenever you feel a need for better communication.

Here are some comments from parents who have used this tool:

"It helped me talk with my husband about disciplining—because this is what I find hardest about parenting our son, Nate. I feel like I am always the one to say no while my husband has all the fun. He thinks I say no to Nate too often, so he concentrates on letting Nate have fun. When we got to the question of how we can best support Nate, we realized he needs to have fun with both of us and to see us both as limit setters. And so we made a plan: During the next week, my husband is going to try to be more of the limit setter, and I'll spend more time playing. We'll see how our plan works for the three of us and take it from there."

"I shared the questionnaire with my son's caregiver, Fahema, at our parent–teacher conference. I said that I thought Marcello was too quiet and needed more help to be assertive and to make friends. When I am with him, like at the playground, he just hangs back and watches rather than play with the other kids. I was amazed to find out that one of the things Fahema said she likes best about Marcello is how well he shares toys with the other kids, letting and even encouraging them to take turns. She also said that Marcello is one of the most well-liked children in the class. I arranged to leave work a little early one day next week so I can spend some time watching Marcello in action. I can't wait to see this!"

Making Decisions Together
Part One: Your Feelings and Reactions

I would use these 10 words to describe (child's name):_____

_____

_____.

What I like most about (child's name) is _____

What I find most challenging about caring for (child's name) is _____

 because_____.

The activity I most enjoy with (child's name) is _____ because

_____.

Three wishes I have for (child's name) are:_____

_____

_____

_____.

Part Two: Tuning in to (child's name)

(Child's name) is happiest when _____.

The kinds of play and activities (child's name) enjoys most are_____.

I think these are favorites because _____.

What upsets (child's name) most is _____.

I think he reacts this way because _____.

To comfort (child's name), I _____.

I think (child's name) greatest strengths are _____.

I think (child's name) needs help with _____.

Part Three: Using What You Know to Decide How Best to Support (child's name)

What are our goals for (child's name) now? During the next 3 months?

What kinds of experiences can we give (child's name) to help him attain these goals?

What special interests or skills do we each have that we each share with and teach (child's name)?

How can we work together to best support (child's name) now? During the next 3 months?

Resolving Differences

It's normal for parents and other caregivers to disagree occasionally about what is best for a child. Even parents of the same child often have different opinions about what the best decision is for their child.

Overlooking Small Differences

Sometimes the issues about which caregivers disagree are small. You feel that you can overlook them, especially if you are confident that the other adult is loving and responsible. For example, you may "let go" of the fact that grandma allows your child to stay up late to catch fireflies. Or you might brush off the fact that your child's clothes were spattered with paint at child care because the caregivers couldn't find her smock.

But sometimes, "letting it go" is not so easy. When young children are concerned, even small issues can stir up strong emotions. One mom told us about feeling furious—and laying into the staff—when the air conditioning in her child's center was broken for 3 days in the middle of a heat wave (although she eventually realized that her child was fine). "I don't think I am a maniac mom," she said, "just one who loves her kid a ton." Another mom talked about her anger at her husband for letting their toddler try to climb the stairs of the slide on her own, even though her husband was right behind their child.

Communicating: The Key to Working It Out

When you do feel strongly that someone caring for your baby or toddler is making a poor decision, you need to talk about your concern—especially when it involves

the physical or emotional health and safety of your child. Whatever the disagreement, communication is the key to resolving differences.

Begin by acknowledging that you and the caregiver each want the best for your child. Then you can use the three-step process to try to listen to one another's perspectives with openness and respect, think together about what the child needs, and decide on a plan. After giving the plan a try, come back together and go through the steps again, adapting your plan as necessary.

Denise drops by the classroom of her 2-year-old son, Tyler, to drop off some diapers. What she sees distresses her. Some of the kids are sitting at the table eating while others, including Tyler, play around the room. Denise asks Lilly, one of the teachers, why all the kids are not sitting down together. Lilly explains that the rule is that, once you are done eating and have cleaned up your space, you may play quietly until everyone is finished.

Denise explains that she doesn't like this rule. At home, Tyler must sit at the table until everyone is done. This practice is very important to Denise and her husband because they see mealtimes as very important family times. They also want Tyler to be well mannered and to learn to wait.

Lilly says she understands why Denise is upset, given her goals for Tyler. Then she explains that center staff members have a different philosophy. They have found that it is very hard for 2-year-olds to wait, and they feel that learning to play quietly and entertain themselves while others finish eating is a good skill for children to develop. Finally, Lilly expresses concern that insisting all the children stay at the table until everyone is finished would turn lunchtime into a struggle for everyone.

Three Steps to Resolving Differences

Because emotions can run so high, a helpful approach is to have a plan in mind about how to handle differences that may arise with your child's caregiver before they actually come up. You may want to share this tool with others who care for your child. As one new mother told us, "Knowing there will be differences and having a plan to deal with them gives me hope that sharing the care can work for me and my baby."

- **Step 1: Be aware of what each of you brings by sharing your feelings and thoughts about the situation.** *Choose a time to meet that works for everyone involved. Make plans, if possible, for another adult to be with your child so you will not be interrupted. Give each person time to share her perspective. While one person is talking, the other listens, reserves judgment, and shows respect for the speaker's perspective.*

- **Step 2: Tune in to your child.** *Share what you know about what is going on in your child's world, his stage of development, and his temperament. Use what you know to think about what your child might be experiencing and what his individual needs are.*

- **Step 3: Decide on a plan that best supports your child.** *Try it out. Arrange a time to meet again to see how things are going, and go through the steps again if necessary.*

Lilly suggests one way to handle this situation: Denise might explain to Tyler that, like at home, he needs to stay in his seat at school until everyone is done eating, and that Lilly and her co-teacher will enforce that. After trying this plan for a week, Lilly shares her observation and concern that it was hard for Tyler to stay at the table when his buddies were allowed to move around, although she does think that, eventually, he might get used to it. He protested and then just put his head down until lunchtime was over. Denise feels badly about her son's reaction. She has also been thinking, since her first discussion with Lilly, that it is good for children to learn to entertain themselves as they wait for others to finish. Because Tyler is a pretty flexible kid, Denise wonders whether he could understand that there are different mealtime rules for home and school. They decide to try it and check in with each other in a few days to see how things are going.

As you might imagine, this process is often easier said than done. When strong emotions are involved, the last thing you may be able to do is sit and listen with an open mind to the person with whom you are upset. In these very charged situations, it may help to talk over your concerns with a third party to give you a chance to calm down, clarify your thoughts and feelings, and gain some perspective. Always remember that the main goal is keeping your child's best interests in the forefront.

Remember—

- No matter how much you love your spouse or trust and respect your child's care provider, sharing the care of a young child can stir up strong feelings. Being aware of these feelings can help you keep them from getting in the way of working together with other adults who also have your child's best interests in mind.

- No one can take your place—not the best-trained, most competent child-care provider in the world, not your spouse, not your partner, not your mother.

- It's normal for parents and other caregivers to disagree occasionally about what is best for a child. Even parents of the same child often have different opinions about what the best decision is for their child.

- Always remember to keep your child's best interests in the forefront when resolving differences.

- Communication is the key to successful partnership with the other adults in your child's life.

CHAPTER 5
Thoughts to Grow On

IN THIS FINAL CHAPTER, WE OFFER A CHART that identifies typical behaviors that you might observe at different stages in your child's early development. The chart also presents possible explanations for what your child may be trying to communicate and suggests ways in which you might want to respond. We encourage you to use what you know about your child to consider whether you have a different interpretation of what a certain behavior might mean for your child, and what your response might be based on that understanding.

You'll see in the chart that the age ranges for developmental milestones are broad. We've done this intentionally because the more we learn about babies, the clearer it is that no two babies develop at the same rate. Development is not a race. It unfolds in stages that can span several months. Whether a baby reaches a milestone earlier or later within the normal timeframe is not significant.

Remember as you read the chart that understanding your child's cues is like being a detective, and that the process takes patience and practice. Using what you know about yourself and your child, and engaging in an ongoing process of trial and error, will help you make the best decisions possible for you and your child.

Birth to 12 Months: Your Remarkable Baby

Chart adapted from Learning & Growing
Together: Understanding and Supporting
Your Child's Development *(2000) by Claire
Lerner and Amy Laura Dombro, and from*
Caring for Infants and Toddlers in Groups:
Developmentally Appropriate Practice
*(2003 edition) by J. Ronald Lally, Abbey Griffin,
Emily Fenichel, Marilyn Segal, Eleanor Szanton,
and Bernice Weissbourd, both published by
ZERO TO THREE, Washington, D.C.*

WHEN YOUR CHILD...

...stops crying because she sees you coming.

...cries, coos, gurgles, whimpers, smiles, rubs his eyes, arches his back, turns his head away, opens his eyes widely.

...startles and cries at loud noises.

...breaks into tears when you arrive to pick him up from child care.

...smiles and responds with pleasure when you talk, sing, or read to her.

...cries or clings to you when a new person approaches.

...observes his own hands; pulls off your glasses; sticks his fingers in your nose; reaches for a toy; grabs the phone.

...holds up her head; turns from stomach to back and from back to stomach; creeps forward or backward; crawls; makes other strides in gross motor development.

...looks up at you and smiles when she has done something great.

...grabs for the spoon while you feed her or smears cooked carrot all over her face, high chair tray, and you.

YOUR CHILD MIGHT BE SAYING:

WHAT YOU CAN DO:

YOUR CHILD MIGHT BE SAYING:	WHAT YOU CAN DO:
I know I can count on you when I need you. I trust your love. Don't worry about spoiling me. When I get what I need when I need it, I feel good about myself and the people around me.	• Respond promptly when she cries. • Look for patterns in her cries and other cues. Is she tired? Wet? Hungry? Bored? Lonely? Overstimulated and in need of a break?
Watch me carefully! I communicate through cries, facial expressions, and movements when I'm sleepy, hungry, wet, frightened, bored, overwhelmed, or interested.	• Trust your instincts when you respond to your baby. His responses will tell you if you're on target. If not, try something else.
I'm sensitive to sounds. Some kids might love loud cars and trucks, but not me. I learn that it's safe to show you how I feel because you comfort me when I'm distressed.	• Acknowledge feelings and offer reassurance: "That fire engine scared you, but you're safe." • Introduce her slowly, in the safety of your arms, to new sounds and places.
When I see you after a long day, I remember how much I've missed you. I save my most intense feelings for you because I trust you. You always come back.	• Don't rush out. Join in finishing what he was doing when you arrived. • Establish a "going home" ritual. Rituals are a comforting way to ease transitions.
I love it when we talk and sing together. When I see how much fun words can be, it makes me want to keep talking and learning.	• Spend lots of time reading together. Let her choose the books, and explore them in any way she pleases. • Talk about whatever you are doing together.
I don't know this person. I don't know what to expect from her, and that scares me.	• Give your child the space and time—in your arms or on your lap—to get used to new people. • Urge others to approach slowly. Have them break the ice by offering an interesting object.
I am learning about how the world works and all of the things I can do with my own hands. I'm pretty amazing!	• Encourage his curiosity by offering safe objects to explore. • Guide his hands gently as he explores your face. • Share his excitement about new discoveries.
I am learning how to make my body do what I want it to do. I'm so thrilled with what I can do that, sometimes, I just can't seem to stop. I want to practice all the time!	• Provide lots of opportunities for her to explore with her body, such as creeping to get an object. • Babyproof your home so that she can move safely and so you don't spend all of your time saying, "No."
Look at me! Look at me! I'm awesome! When I know that you're proud, too, it makes me eager to try new things.	• Share her pleasure in her accomplishments. • Create opportunities for her to master new skills.
I want to feed myself. The more things I do for myself, the better I feel!	• Offer safe finger foods and a child's spoon to hold and practice using as you feed her. • Forget about mess! Use big bibs, bathe her after dinner, and put a rubber mat under the highchair.

12 to 24 Months: Your Young Exlorer

WHEN YOUR CHILD...

...protests at bedtime.

...clings or cries when you are leaving.

...makes marks with crayons, stacks blocks, uses a spoon, drinks from a cup, and does other things using her small motor skills.

...responds to music by dancing, moving, and brightening up.

...toddles over after venturing off on his own and grabs your legs.

...points to something and then looks at you to share her discovery.

...says, "No!" and starts challenging rules and pushing limits.

...sometimes act like he's going on 15 and at other times acts like a baby again.

Chart adapted from Learning & Growing Together: Understanding and Supporting Your Child's Development *(2000) by Claire Lerner and Amy Laura Dombro, and from* Caring for Infants and Toddlers in Groups: Developmentally Appropriate Practice *(2003 edition) by J. Ronald Lally, Abbey Griffin, Emily Fenichel, Marilyn Segal, Eleanor Szanton, and Bernice Weissbourd, both published by ZERO TO THREE, Washington, D.C.*

YOUR CHILD MIGHT BE SAYING:	WHAT YOU CAN DO:
There are too many exciting things going on. And I want to stay with you.	• Tell him when bedtime is approaching. • Establish a regular bedtime routine: bath, bed, book…or whatever sequence works. • Give him a sense of control; let him pick the book or song.
I love you. You make me feel safe. I can't bear the idea of your leaving because I need you for so many things.	• Remind yourself that separations are difficult. • Play games such as peekaboo to prepare him for separation. • When you say, "Good-bye," calmly reassure him that you will always come back.
I am learning to use my hands to explore and do things for myself. I'm so proud of what I can do! It helps me learn about all kinds of new things.	• Offer objects such as spoons, cups, and safe but small toys that give her a chance to practice using her fingers. • Teach her how meaningful her activities are. Send her scribbles in a letter to grandma. Have her help with cleaning up, now that she's able.
This sounds great! I love to move, move, move!	• Join in, laugh, and dance. • Listen to all kinds of music. See what she likes best.
No matter where I go, you'll always be there for me. You're my home base. As I venture off, I know I can always return to you.	• Greet your returning traveler with a big hug that lets him know you love him. • Play disappearing/reappearing games such as hide and seek. They will help him cope with separations.
Look at what I discovered. I want to see it or smell it or hold it. Can you get it for me so I can touch it, smell it, taste it?	• Talk about her discoveries and lift her to see, smell, or touch them. • If it's safe, offer her the object to explore.
I am a person with my own ideas. I am learning who I am and how to behave by trying out different ways and seeing which works best.	• Encourage independence with limited choices: "Red or blue sweater?" not "Which sweater?" • Establish consistent limits. • Maintain a sense of humor.
I want to be grown-up and independent, but sometimes I get scared and need to know you're there for me. Try to be patient. This isn't easy for me, either!	• Be flexible. Support his independence, but let him revisit babyhood. • Let him help with real work, such as setting the table, so that he can feel "big." • Maintain special rituals from babyhood—for example, a bedtime routine.

24 Months to 3 Years: Your Independent, Competent Toddle

WHEN YOUR CHILD...

...has trouble knowing when to stop.

...hits, pushes, or bites another child.

...has a temper tantrum.

...plays pretend games with stuffed animals or make-believe toys such as telephones, cars, or dress-up clothes.

Chart adapted from Learning & Growing Together: Understanding and Supporting Your Child's Development *(2000) by Claire Lerner and Amy Laura Dombro, and from* Caring for Infants and Toddlers in Groups: Developmentally Appropriate Practice *(2003 edition) by J. Ronald Lally, Abbey Griffin, Emily Fenichel, Marilyn Segal, Eleanor Szanton, and Bernice Weissbourd, both published by* ZERO TO THREE, Washington, D.C.

YOUR CHILD MIGHT BE SAYING:	**WHAT YOU CAN DO:**
I can't always put the brakes on when I am having a great time. Sometimes the things I'm doing are so-o-o exciting! With your help, I'll learn about self-control, but don't expect it to happen overnight.	• Establish clear rules and stick to them: "Balls are for outside." "All food and drinks at the table." Expect that he'll need reminders. • Always acknowledge when he shows self-control: "You remembered to bring your milk to the table. Good job!"
I'm angry, frustrated, or maybe just overexcited. I can't control myself. Help me, please!	• Watch for rising tension and signs of potential conflict. Step in before things get out of control. • Acknowledge feelings: "You're angry that Jake took your cookie." • Be clear about acceptable behavior: "It's okay to be angry, but it's not okay to hit."
I've lost control. Maybe it's because I'm frustrated, tired, or angry. Or maybe I'm just overwhelmed by too much going on around me, and I need a break.	• Look for patterns to figure out what triggers his tantrums. • When it's over, put his feelings into words, and make a plan next time: "You got frustrated putting your shoe on. Next time you can ask for help."
I'm practicing being a grown-up by doing things just like you. In my imagination, I can do anything and be anyone. That's the best part of play.	• Encourage imaginary play by providing lots of props and joining in. • Follow her lead and don't take over. You're a visitor in her world—she knows the rules!

Continued

24 Months to 3 Years   Continued

WHEN YOUR CHILD...

...wants to play more and more with other children.

...has trouble sharing or taking turns.

...throws a ball, stands on one foot, walks up the stairs, eats with a spoon and fork, pours milk on her cereal, and pulls on her own shirt and pants.

...tells you when his diaper is wet, or runs to the potty and sits on it fully clothed.

...gets frustrated trying to express herself.

...wants you to read the same stories over and over.

Chart adapted from Learning & Growing Together: Understanding and Supporting Your Child's Development *(2000) by Claire Lerner and Amy Laura Dombro, and from* Caring for Infants and Toddlers in Groups: Developmentally Appropriate Practice *(2003 edition) by J. Ronald Lally, Abbey Griffin, Emily Fenichel, Marilyn Segal, Eleanor Szanton, and Bernice Weissbourd, both published by ZERO TO THREE, Washington, D.C.*

YOUR CHILD MIGHT BE SAYING:

WHAT YOU CAN DO:

YOUR CHILD MIGHT BE SAYING:	WHAT YOU CAN DO:
I like to play with people who look and act like me. I learn by watching what they do; and when I play with them, they become my special friends.	• Provide lots of opportunities for interaction with peers. • Know your child and what her ideal play situation is—for example: how long before she gets tired, how many friends to play with at once, what the best time of day is for playdates.
I'm beginning to learn that things aren't always the way I want them to be. It will take me a while and lots of practice to develop these skills.	• Let older toddlers try to work things out for themselves before stepping in to help. • Be their sharing coach. Help them take turns.
I'm getting to be very grown up. I can do so many things for myself. Sometimes I don't want any help from you. But I never mind hearing how terrific you think I am.	• As your toddler grows, let him do more for himself. Put a stool near the sink so he can brush his teeth. Let him select his clothing and help sort laundry. It all builds self-esteem.
I know just what's happening in my body, and I'm thinking about starting to use this potty.	• Follow his lead. Forcing can lead to resistance and power struggles. • Expect lots of interest in potty activities, including company when you go to the bathroom. • Expect accidents, and never punish him for them. Treat such situations matter-of-factly.
I can't always figure out how to say what I mean. Sometimes I stumble on my words because I can't get them out as fast as I want.	• Acknowledge her frustration. • Be patient and listen carefully. • Offer words for what she may be trying to say: "Are you sad that you dropped your ice-pop?"
This story is like an old friend. It makes me feel safe and secure. I like knowing what to expect, and I love knowing what all the words mean. Pretty soon, I'll tell you the story and you can listen.	• Honor her requests when she asks for a story. • Leave out the last word of a sentence and see if she fills it in. • Change a word and see if she corrects you. • When you just can't bear reading that same book again, ask her to "read" it to you, or to a special doll or stuffed animal.

Promoting Your Child's Healthy Development Day by Day

Every day, you make hundreds of decisions—some small, some big. As you try to make the best decisions possible for your child and for yourself, remember that you already do a great deal to support your child's development as you lovingly care for her every day. So have fun! Share and delight in your child's discoveries. Go on outdoor explorations. Allow her to discover the beauty of the surrounding world—worms slither, dry leaves crackle under our feet, snow is cold. Talk about what you are doing together. Cuddle with lots of good books. Share music and dance together. Watch your child and listen to her.

Try to see the world through your child's eyes to understand her interests as well as her frustrations. And love your little one as much as you can; some days may seem long, but those first 3 years are very short!

Understanding Development Through Your Child's Eyes

THIS CHART SHOWS HOW DEVELOPMENT PROGRESSES in the first 3 years. It can help you identify where your child is along a developmental pathway and what next steps he might be ready to take. Most babies follow the same sequence of developmental steps (using gestures to communicate before they use words), but no two babies develop at the same rate. Whether a baby reaches a milestone earlier or later within the normal time frame isn't significant.

The chart is divided into three age ranges: birth to 12 months, 12 to 24 months, and 24 to 36 months. After each section, you will find answers to some common questions that parents have at that stage of development. (Adapted with permission from articles by Claire Lerner in *American Baby* magazine.)

Birth to 12 Months

I Learn About What My Body Can Do

- Sucking soothes me.

- I recognize the smell and voices of those caring for me the most.

- In the first 2 months, I can focus best on things that are 8–12 inches away.

- I turn my head or close my eyes when it is too bright.

- I connect sounds with their sources. My favorite sound is the human voice.

- I have a good grip as a newborn. I will hold onto things you put in my hand. At about 3 months, I will start to reach and grasp things with both my hands.

- I will learn to hold my head up, roll, and probably crawl. I have favorite positions, but it's good for me to be on my belly, back, and sitting up so I can see things from different perspectives and learn to move in different ways. I can stand if I have something to hold onto, and I may even start to walk. (But remember, I should always sleep on my back!)

continued

Birth to 12 Months *continued*

I Learn About My Feelings and Who I Am

• I feel secure when you hold me, smile at me, and talk with me.

• Sometimes I startle, get frightened, or have taken in too much stimulation, and I need help to settle down.

• I learn to comfort myself. I may suck on my fingers or hands.

• I can show you many feelings. I smile and wiggle to show you that I like playing with you. I frown or cry when you stop playing with me. I arch my back and turn away when I need a break from playing or interacting.

• By 4–6 months, if you watch closely, you can begin to see what makes me unique—my likes and dislikes, my interests, how I like to interact, how I deal with change.

I Learn About People, Objects, and How Things Work

• I love to play games like peek-a-boo with you. When I want you to keep playing, I wave my arms and legs and make sounds to let you know I don't want you to stop.

• I learn I can make things happen. I can shake a rattle and make a sound. I can kick a mobile and make it move. I can smile, and you will smile back.

• By 6 months, I can tell the difference between people I do and don't know. Sometimes, I may be afraid of strangers.

• By 8 or 9 months, I might like to explore my food and even feed myself with my hands. It might get pretty messy at times, but it helps me feel confident.

I Learn to Communicate and Relate

• I have different cries, facial expressions, and body movements to tell you that I am sleepy, hungry, wet, scared, uncomfortable, overwhelmed, or even bored and want to play.

• I move my arms and legs, I smile and gurgle, when I am happy and excited.

• Between 3 and 4 months, I begin to really enjoy babbling to you. I'll begin with open vowels (oohs and ahs) and move to new sounds and combinations, with P's, M's, B's, and D's.

• I will start to imitate the sounds that you make. My babbling may even start to sound like your speech. My voice might go up as if I'm asking a question. It may sound like I am saying a whole sentence.

• I learn about words and the joys of language when you talk, sing, and read with me.

My 3-week-old son wants to be held all the time. I can't put him down without him crying within 5 or 10 minutes. He sleeps with me at night, and other than that, he only naps if someone is holding him. I've tried white noise and swings, and they don't work.

As tough as it can be sometimes for new parents who just want a few minutes to themselves (or even—dare we say it—the bliss of a solo bathroom break), the fact is that very young babies often prefer being held than being in any other position. This makes sense from an evolutionary standpoint—staying close to your source of food and protection is pretty savvy.

And being cuddled up with the people who love you meets other important needs that very young children have. When you hold your son, he feels your body warmth and hears your heartbeat—a familiar sound from inside the womb. He smells your scent. When you cuddle him curled up close he feels safe; it reminds him of the good old days back inside your belly. Plus, the closer he is, the more

likely he is to be on the receiving end of your care and kisses; you're more likely to rub his bald little head, kiss his perfectly chubby cheeks, or let him wrap his tiny hand around your index finger. So at this point in your sons' life, it's developmentally on-target for him to want to be with you—held by you—as much as possible.

So, what can you do to get the breaks you need? Some parents find that a baby carrier or sling is a good compromise. They don't have to physically hold the baby, but they can still keep them close while getting things done around the house. My daughter sounds a lot like your son, and I remember marveling at the fact that even as I bobbed up and down while unloading the dishwasher, she never made a peep while I wore her in the baby carrier. This is also the perfect time to call some of those people who offered to help with the baby—friends, family, neighbors, or a postpartum doula—to come over for an hour or two to hold your son while you shower, send a few e-mails, run an errand or two, or just collapse into bed for a nap.

As far as your son's napping goes, because he sleeps with you at night, he is probably pretty used to falling asleep next to another warm body. You can either continue this during the day by letting him fall asleep in a baby carrier or sling, or you can help him begin learning how to sleep on his own. To do this, you can try swaddling him (to mimic the feeling of being held) and then putting him down; but stay with him and rock him, sing, or stroke his face or hand until he calms down. Babies at this age simply don't have the ability to calm themselves so it's important *not* to let him just "cry it out." Instead, stay with him and do the things that will help him calm himself. And, of course, if your intuition is telling you to pick him up, that's fine.

It will take time for your son to learn to fall asleep on his own; it's a skill that he will spend most of his first 6 months to a year mastering. So be patient, seek help when you need it and, even as you fantasize about a *whole 30 minutes alone*, realize that these early days and months fly by so quickly. Before you know it, your son will learn to crawl and you'll be running to catch up with him! (And by the time he's 11 and 13—like my kids— you'll be begging *him* for cuddles.)

I am a working mom of a 9-month-old baby girl, and I feel really stressed about not having the time to teach her all the things I read about that she should be learning. I want to help her learn, but I also just want to have fun with her for the few hours I have with her each day. We have lots of educational toys for her, but she seems to like everyday things better, like playing in the bath. What's more important for her, fun or learning?

I'm so glad you asked, because I have really good news for you: It turns out that not only are fun and learning both very important, but they are linked. Children learn best when the learning is fun, when it happens during the normal course of the day, and when it emerges from the world around them. And very young children learn best when the adults in their world follow their lead and teach them new skills through their natural interests— for example, teaching a child about big and small by comparing the two rubber duckies in the tub. You don't have to create special, structured activities with "make your baby smarter" videos, flashcards, and the like. Research shows that children get all the stimulation they need from life itself. They enter the world ready to learn and driven to walk, talk, speak, love, and explore. You support their natural passion for learning by making the most of daily experiences and routines. Let's look at how bathtime can be a powerful learning experience for your child.

First, this is a time when your entire focus is on your daughter, perhaps more than at any other time of day because you need to be right there with her to make sure she is safe. She feels your gentle touch during the bath and later as you cuddle her up in a towel. While you wash her, you talk about what you're doing. Perhaps you a sing a song: "Head and shoulders, knees and toes, knees and toes…" When you stop, your daughter laughs, kicks her arms and legs excitedly, and makes happy babbles. You continue to sing, and she beams a wide smile at you. She picks up a bucket full of water. You put rubber duckie into it. She pours him out. You pick him up and put him back in. She laughs and dumps him back out. You pick up the soap and drop it to the bottom of the tub. She looks around, finds it, and picks it up. Another game has begun.

Think of all that she is learning! You nurture her social and emotional development as your undivided attention and gentle touch let her know that she is very important and loved. As you play together, she sees herself as someone others like to be with. Your baby also learns how to engage others when you respond to her overtures. And the back-and-forth games that you play help her learn to take turns and to be a good playmate and friend as she grows.

You promote her communication skills when you understand and respond to her gestures and vocalizations. You are telling her that she is worth listening to and that she has important things to say. This lets her know she is a good communicator, which makes her want to communicate more and more.

Your play in the tub encourages her intellectual development when she experiences cause and effect by kicking her legs and feeling the water splash. By singing songs, she learns new words. When you play with the bucket, the water, the duckie, and the soap, she learns math and science concepts such as full and empty, floating and sinking, and the difference between liquids and solids. The searching-for-the-soap game also helps her master the concept of object permanence—that things exist even though she can't see them.

Taking a bath—as simple as it seems—offers children a rich and meaningful learning experience. It is a wonderful opportunity to nurture a strong, loving relationship between you and your child (as are other everyday routines like diapering, feeding, and putting your child to bed). So let the pressure go—and appreciate the magic of everyday moments.

My 8-month-old is often in the same room as my two older children, a preschooler and a kindergartner, while they're watching TV. I see the baby reacting excitedly to the images on the screen. Is all that inadvertent TV watching bad for him?

You raise a fascinating question, and one that more and more researchers are beginning to examine. Unfortunately, there hasn't yet been any definitive research on the impact of television viewing on children younger than 2, whether it is direct or indirect exposure. But stay tuned: Researchers are actively working on answering this and other important questions about the media's effect on children.

Although we don't know the exact impact that indirect or "background" viewing has on your child, we do know a lot about how children take in information and learn. Even though your child may not be sitting down directly in front of the television, he may be exposed to images that are scary or confusing to him, and the quick "cuts" from scene to scene may be overstimulating. In addition, it can be a distraction from his focus on playing, which is much more important for his development than watching TV. The background noise may also discourage your child's "talking" to himself during play, which is a very important way in which young children develop good language skills.

Even "educational" shows may have little value for children 2 and younger. Children learn best from "doing," and from taking in information as they live their daily lives. For example, it is more meaningful and lasting when children learn about big and small as they explore rocks during a walk in the neighborhood, or learn colors as they help you sort laundry, than by viewing a children's television segment on these concepts.

The primary concern with television viewing is that it takes place at the expense of parental interaction and other activities like creative play, exercise, and reading books—all fun, interactive experiences that help build important social–emotional, language, and cognitive skills. In addition, if children begin at an early age to depend on TV for entertainment, parents may find it increasingly difficult to limit viewing as their children get older.

To help you make good decisions about TV watching for your children, consider the following:

- Closely monitor what your baby sees on television and try to limit his viewing to no more than 30 minutes per day.

- Join him when he's watching TV.

- Find other activities that will engage your baby when you need a break. Provide him with a basket of toys that can be used for independent play (e.g., books, blocks, balls) while you prepare dinner, pay the bills, or lie down on the couch for some R&R.

- When your older children are watching TV, take your baby with you to another part of the house. Make that a "special time" to talk with him and play together.

With this in mind, it is important to maintain some perspective. TV watching, within appropriate limits, often provides both parent and child with a much-needed break. Parents can also extend the value of what children are taking in from the shows they are watching by linking what they learn to daily life. For example, if your child is interested in a show about animals, you can go to the zoo and help him identify animals he knows, and read books together about those animals.

The overall goal is to ensure that TV viewing doesn't distract your little learner from other, more beneficial forms of play that will enhance his growth and development throughout the infant–toddler years.

I am a mom of a newborn. French is my native language. I have heard conflicting opinions on speaking both French and English with her—some say it's good, others say that it can delay language development. What should I do?

Go for it. Exposing your baby to a natural and rich environment in both English and French will help her become bilingual before she ever begins any formal education. And by providing your baby the opportunity to learn the language of your family's culture, you are contributing to the development of her identity by passing on a sense of connection to her family's roots and as you share a unique language relationship together.

There is still a lot of research to be done on childhood bilingualism. What we do know is that children can learn two or more languages during childhood without any problems. We also know that, in fact, it is much easier to learn language in the early years. Parents should keep in mind the following variables that impact bilingual development:

- Babies learn at their own individual *pace*. So your child may develop her language skills at a different rate than a monolingual child, and it may have nothing to do with the fact that she is learning two languages at once. Further, research shows that children who are exposed to a rich bilingual language environment on a regular basis follow a similar *course* of language acquisition as monolingual children.

- A key variable for bilingual acquisition is consistency in *how* children are exposed to the two languages throughout their early childhood. You can choose to provide consistency in a variety of ways. For example, you might speak only French to her while Dad speaks only English. Or, only French is spoken in the home and English outside the home. An important consideration for parents living in communities where the non-English language is *not* supported is to provide children with lots of non-English-language experiences in the home to compensate.

- Be aware that your child may develop her vocabulary at a different rate than a monolingual child. Children learning two languages simultaneously may have smaller vocabularies in one or both languages compared to children learning only one language. However, when both languages are taken into consideration, bilingual children tend to have the same number of words as monolinguals. Keep in mind that these initial differences are temporary, assuming that the child is provided with an optimal bilingual language environment. The good news is that with the consistency in language use, as well as hearing both languages spoken on a regular basis, by the time they enter school they catch up.

Remember that if the goal for your child is bilingualism and biliteracy, it is critical that you provide her with rich, natural, constant, and varied language experiences that support the development of both languages. Don't worry about your child getting confused by the exposure to and use of two languages. She will begin to sort it out on her own, and even sometimes use words from both languages in the same sentence. This does *not* mean she is mixed up! It is a very normal part of the bilingual childhood experience. So delight in the joy of hearing your child explore and master two languages. What a gift you are giving her.

I have a 9-month-old daughter who used to eat anything, but now when I try to feed her vegetables she clamps her lips shut, cries, and pushes the spoon away. When we give her fruit or open the cereal box, all of a sudden her legs start kicking, her eyes get wide, and she opens her mouth as wide as can be. What can I do to make sure she has a well-balanced diet and eats the veggies? Every mealtime is turning into a huge battle, and my husband and I are starting to dread feeding her.

Have no fear. There are so many babies who do this, and so many parents who worry about it, that I have consulted with several pediatricians about what parents should do in this situation. And here's what they tell me: Your baby will be just fine. She is getting all the nutrients and calories she needs from fruits, cereal, and milk (be it breast or formula).

So you don't have to worry about your daughter's physical health. In fact, her behavior is actually letting you know that she is doing very well in many key areas of her development. She knows what she likes and doesn't like, and she is able to effectively communicate that to you. When you read and respond to her cues—in this case, by not forcing her to eat what she is telling you she doesn't want—you are teaching her that her feelings are important, and that she is a good communicator, which will help build her self-esteem and encourage her to develop good language skills as she grows.

It is important to avoid getting into power struggles that can develop around food when children are discriminating eaters (which accounts for many children. You are not alone!). This may change as your daughter grows, but she may never be one of those kids who are willing to try and then enjoy everything that comes their way. When parents get anxious that their children are not eating enough, there is the risk that they will begin to force the child to eat. This can lead to several problems, including:

- *Actually eating less.* Research shows that letting children decide what and how much they want to eat leads to their eating more food than those who are forced.

- *Negative impact on the parent–child relationship.* Children pick up on their parents' frustration and internalize feelings that they (the children) are unacceptable. This can lead to more negative behaviors as the child "fulfills the prophecy" that she is "trouble." Also, when there are power struggles around feeding, it is more likely that there will be similar struggles over other issues as the child grows.

- *An increased chance that the child will have struggles with food later.* When a child's cues are disregarded by her parents and they force her to eat, she may learn that her feelings are not important and that she can't trust her body's cues. This can lead to difficulty knowing when she is hungry and full, which can then lead to eating disorders and obesity later in life.

My advice is to talk with your pediatrician to get the assurance that your child is growing fine. Many pediatricians suggest that parents give their child a multivitamin so that they don't have to worry. (Usually this vitamin is not necessary, but it helps manage parents' anxiety!)

Once you are reassured that your child will be fine without eating the vegetables, here are some strategies that you can try over time to encourage your child to eat and enjoy a broader range of foods. Again remember that these are not necessary for her health, but more for her lifestyle and adaptability.

- Help your child feel more in control by encouraging her to help you hold the spoon to feed herself.

- Offer lots of different foods (in small portions!), and offer the new food *before* you give her the old favorites.

- Don't give up on new foods. Research has shown that you should offer a food 13 times before a child knows whether she likes it or not!

- As she grows, you can make mealtime and food fun by allowing acceptable choices and having her help prepare—mixing, spreading butter on bread, etc.

- Give her positive reinforcement for trying something new. "You tried the green beans. I'm so proud of you for trying!"

So sit back and relax. Remember that mealtime is also a time for communicating and bonding. Making mealtime an enjoyable experience for *both* you and your baby is key to ensuring that she gets the nutrition she needs, and it will help her develop healthy eating habits as she grows.

12 to 24 Months

I Learn About What My Body Can Do

- I can make marks on paper with crayons. I can stack and line up blocks. I can feed myself with my fingers. If you encourage me, I can use a spoon and can drink from a cup.

- I can crawl, then walk, then run! I love to try to climb stairs but still need a lot of help with this.

- I want to help you get me dressed and undressed. I can push my foot into my shoe and my arm into my sleeve.

I Learn About My Feelings and Who I Am

- I feel important and loved when you listen to, talk to, and play with me; when you love and cuddle me; when you encourage me to explore and join in my discoveries; when you show that you are proud of me.

- I have favorite people, toys, food, and clothing.

- I can point to and tell you the names of many parts of my body. I begin to use "me" and "mine."

- I have strong feelings and may express them with gusto. I might say "No!" a lot or give orders, like telling you to "Sit there!" to show you I know what I want and that I have a mind of my own.

- Separations are hard. I may even cry when I see you again after we have been apart because I've missed you so much.

- I like to make choices. Doing so helps me feel that I am competent and that I have some control.

- Routines help me know what to expect and to feel safe and secure.

- I can get frustrated and angry pretty easily because there are so many things I want to do that I can't do yet. I may push, hit, or bite. I need you to help me manage my strong feelings, but it will still take time for me to learn better self-control.

- Even though I understand when you tell me "No!" or "Stop!" I still can't keep myself from doing things I shouldn't.

- One minute I might act really independent. The next, I act like a little baby who needs you to do everything for me. Being a "big kid" can feel scary sometimes. I need to know that you or someone else I can trust are always there to care for me.

continued

12 to 24 Months *continued*

I Learn About People, Objects, and How Things Work

- I like to be with other children, but kids my age still don't know how to share. You can help us learn to take turns.

- I imitate you. I see how you talk with other people and how you do things like cleaning, caring for the dog, cooking dinner, fixing things around the house.

- I am a little scientist. I want to explore during every waking moment so I can figure out how everything works—from how to get you to read my favorite book to how to make the block fit in the hole or how to make my music box start again.

- Separations can be really hard. Seeing that you always come back will help make separations easier over time.

I Learn to Communicate and Relate

- I use my body, sounds, words, and facial expressions to let you know what I am thinking and feeling.

- I point to show you what interests me, so you'll look too and tell me about what I see.

- I create long babble sentences. I may be able to say a few words or use consistent sounds for words, like "baba" for bottle. I may push the cracker that I don't want off the high chair and say "nuh-nuh."

- I understand a lot more than I can say. I can follow simple directions like "Go get your ball."

- I imitate what you say. So don't be surprised if you hear the words you use coming out of my mouth.

My 18-month old has loved up her stuffed bunny so much that it's literally falling apart—and it smells bad! I want to get rid of it, but I'm worried about how my baby will react. I can't find another bunny that's exactly like it to replace it. Is there a way to get her to prefer a new toy or a different stuffed bunny?

Imagine how you would feel if someone said they were going to take away your beloved spouse/partner/best friend (falling apart and bad-smelling or not!) and get you a new, improved version. Now you know how your child would feel if you replaced her treasured bunny!

"Loveys," *especially* those that are smelly and worn, are very special for children and are a substitute for when they can't have you. Children are so attached to them because they invest in them all the love and security they feel with you. So when they can't have you, they have the next best thing—their beloved lovey! As you've probably seen, your daughter's bunny helps her cope during stressful or scary times, comforts her when she has a boo-boo, gives her something familiar to rely on when she is feeling overwhelmed, and provides support during daily transitions—during drop-off at child care, or from waking to sleeping at night. Also, as your child grows and begins to use words, sometimes her bunny will help her to express her feelings and emotions. She may tell you why the bunny is scared to go to preschool or why the bunny no longer wants to sleep in his room at night by himself.

My suggestion is—don't get rid of it! It is serving a critical role in your daughter's ability to cope with life's challenges. And it's highly unlikely that any replacement will do. (When my son, Sam, was about 9 months old, we left his lovey—an elephant—on a plane and bought him the exact same one when we realized it was gone. Sam immediately stroked its trunk—which had already worn thin on the original—and promptly threw it across the room.)

Here's what you can try, but there are no guarantees:

- Suggest that bunny needs a bath and let them take a bath together. It may not have the same effect as the washing machine but it may be an improvement.

- If you are concerned that bunny may fall apart, suggest that bunny may want a friend. Go to the store and let your daughter choose the friend. Then include the new "friend" in as many ways you can (when you read books and sing together, when you comfort your child, as company on a car ride, etc.) so that hopefully the feelings your daughter has for bunny will transfer to the friend. Then this friend can serve as a substitute when and if bunny does fall apart, although it is more likely that she will simply choose to carry bunny's disembodied ear around rather than accept a replacement. GOOD LUCK!

- Let your child help you as you carefully stitch up bunny. Talk to her about the importance of taking care of herself and others, and use it as an opportunity to start showing her what empathy is all about.

When is it time to say good-bye to loveys? When your child is ready. My experience is that if you don't interfere in their "relationship" and force a separation, children gradually separate on their own. By the time children are school age, the loveys become less central in their lives and usually stay in their beds for nighttime comfort. My kids—now 11 and 13—still have their loveys in their beds and still have very warm, special feelings toward them. (We actually retrieved Sam's original elephant.) The loveys serve as comforting, positive symbols of their childhood.

I'm going back to work and sending my 12-month-old to daycare. How can I get her ready?

The most important first step in preparing a child for going to child care is to ensure that you've selected a place that's right for *your child*—one that best matches her individual needs. For example, if you have a child who gets easily overwhelmed when there is a lot going on around her, it would likely be best for her to be in a center where the classes are small or in a family child-care setting. In general, it is best for young children to be in settings where caregivers adapt schedules to allow children to eat and sleep based on their own daily rhythms; are sensitive and responsive to the individual needs of each child; welcome parent involvement; and provide you with information about your child on a daily basis. When you feel comfortable about the care your child will be receiving, it's much easier to share that same confidence and enthusiasm with your son or daughter.

Once you've selected the best care for your child, there are a number of things you can do to get her off to a good start:

- Plan for brief—and then incrementally longer—separations from you, so that she learns that she can be safe and well cared for by other loving adults. This is especially important if she hasn't spent much time with other caregivers during this first year.

- Take her to the child-care setting several times before her first day to help her become familiar with it. (The unknown is often what is most scary.) Let her explore the classroom and outside play area, and interact with the caregivers and children.

- Read books with her about other children going to child care and dealing with separations.

- Play disappearing/reappearing games such as peek-a-boo and hide-and-seek to help her understand that although things and people may go away, they come back. Emphasize the message that "Mommy may go away, but Mommy always comes back."

- Make an audiotape of yourself reading stories and singing songs for your child to listen to at child care when she misses you.

On your child's first day, you can try a few of the following ideas to make her transition smoother:

- Give her a picture of you and other family members (maybe even the family pet) to look at when she is sad. Ask the caregivers if your daughter can keep these photos in her cubby or somewhere else that's easily accessible to her.

- Allow her to bring a "lovey"—a blanket, doll, or stuffed animal that brings her comfort and is a connection to home.

- When it's time for you to leave her, don't linger or show worry. Children look to the trusted adults in their lives for cues on how to interpret situations. When we look and act worried and upset, our children naturally think there is something to be worried and upset about, and are therefore likely to have a harder time separating. Studies actually show that when parents say a brief, upbeat good-bye, their children stop crying and adjust more quickly. If you are really worried about how your child is faring without you, some child-care centers have "observation rooms" with one-way mirrors where you can watch for a few moments before leaving for work. Or, you can ask the caregivers to call you briefly, just to reassure you that she is doing fine.

- Make sure that you say good-bye to her when you leave. As tempting as it may be to sneak out, hoping that it will ease the transition, your child may experience this as a breach of trust. Sneaking out also sends the message that you feel you are doing something wrong or bad by leaving her. Instead, give her the clear message that she will be fine, and that you look forward to seeing her when you come back.

Finally, don't forget yourself in this transition. You're likely to experience a range of emotions related to separating from your child and sharing her care with others. It's important to pay attention to your own reactions to this separation so that you can deal with your feelings in a thoughtful, productive way. Both you and your child are embarking on a new adventure, one that will have its own challenges but also its own rewards, as your child's world expands and she is enriched by new relationships and experiences.

My daughter (13 months) and I go to a playgroup once a week. Things were fine when the babies were little, but now they are walking around, exploring . . . and grabbing and pushing and hitting! Last week, my daughter grabbed a car out of her friend's hands. Her friend started to cry, and when I made my daughter give the car back, *she* started to cry. It was a mess. When do you start making little kids share? And how?

Hmm... I'm not sure I am the expert on this, as just the other day I had a similar experience—not with toddlers, but with my own 11- and 13-year-olds. What I can tell you is that learning to share is a process—one that *can start* at 13 months but one that takes a long time to master.

So have no fear: The incident you described is very typical. In fact, it's what we expect at this age. Young toddlers are very smart, determined beings who know what they want and are dead set on getting it. Unfortunately, what they don't yet have are the words to express their strong feelings, so they communicate through action. Children at this age are also self-centered, meaning that they do not yet have the capacity to put themselves in other people's shoes or to imagine what others might be feeling. This is why it is hard for them to share. They only know what they feel, not what others feel. They are not thinking, "I really want that car, but grabbing it will make Sherri feel bad." They are more likely thinking, "I want that car and I want it now!" A final complicating factor is that 13-month-olds don't yet have the impulse control to stop themselves from doing something they want to do, even if they have been corrected countless times. For all of these reasons, most children do not learn to share until they are much closer to 2–3 years old.

However, you certainly don't have to wait—and you shouldn't wait—until your child is 2 to start helping her learn to share. Use the countless opportunities during your everyday interactions to work on this. When you are playing, help her take turns. She adds a block, then you add one. At clean-up time, take turns putting the toys back on the shelf. At bedtime, take turns flipping the pages. Through these interactions, your daughter will experience turn-taking as part of a positive, loving relationship that sets the stage for sharing in other relationships.

There are also lots of opportunities to teach about sharing when she is with other children. Learning to get along with others and experiencing the joy of social connections begins in early childhood and lays the foundation for future healthy, successful relationships. The more experience your daughter has with peers, the better—especially when you are there to mediate. Here are some things you can start doing now to help:

- Before a friend comes over, let your child choose the things that are most special and too hard to share—and let her put them away.

- Provide several of the same kinds of toys so that there are enough for everyone.

- Compliment her when she is playing cooperatively and sharing. "I like how you gave Ellie the doll that she wanted."

- Join her play and be her guide. Let her know that you understand how hard it is to share. Tell her that grabbing is not okay, and offer alternatives such as helping her choose another toy in the meantime.

- Keep the turns short and use a timer to help her know when her turn will come. (Often, children become so amused by the idea of the timer that they forget about the "fight.")

- As your daughter grows, include her in the problem-solving. When she and a friend are having trouble sharing, ask for their ideas on a fair resolution. The more involved kids are in decision making, the more invested they are in the follow-through. This also lets your daughter know that you believe she can learn to solve her own challenges—a very important life skill.

My 16-month-old is in that phase when he wants to do everything by himself—from opening a lollipop wrapper to pouring his milk. He's too little to do some things without making a mess or getting hurt—he even wants to cut his own food with the knife! How can I reason with him?

You can't. Sixteen-month-olds are not rational beings, so forget any strategies that include reasoning! What you can and should do is congratulate yourself. You have obviously nurtured in your son an eagerness to learn and a strong sense of self-confidence—two key ingredients for all aspects of his healthy development. Indeed, curious, confident kids can also be a handful as, just like you describe, they want to do everything by themselves. The second year of life is all about making an impact on the world (while wrecking havoc along the way). The good news is that there is a lot you can do to encourage his sense of competence and mastery while also keeping him safe and you sane.

- **Get your creative juices flowing.** Find ways for your child to practice new skills, within limits. For example, if he wants to pour his own milk, offer to do it with him. If he won't let you do this, consider taking the milk and cup outside and letting him do it on his own so you don't have to worry about the mess. If that's not acceptable, you can insist on pouring the milk for him; but later, give him lots of containers that he can pour and empty out in the bathtub. This may fulfill some need to fill and empty; it will also provide lots of good practice so that he will one day be able to pour the milk on his own.

- **Compromise.** If he wants to feed himself, but you don't have all day to wait for him to get an ounce of food in, you can give him a spoon while you use another spoon to get the majority of the meal in his mouth.

- **Find safe alternatives.** There will certainly be times when you have to just say "No." Setting these kinds of limits is your job. You can explain, "These sharp knives are for Mommy and Daddy to use." Then show him how he can use his hands to break up certain foods (my 13-year-old still uses his finger to cut his waffles into pieces!) or help him use a safe, blunt, plastic knife.

- **Be his coach.** When he gets frustrated because he can't do it "all by myself," label his feelings: "It makes you so mad when you can't open the jar!" And introduce him to the word "help." Then provide the assistance he needs to master the challenge without doing it all for him. This may mean holding your hand over his as you unscrew the top; it leaves him feeling like he has been a part of the solution. This will bolster his confidence and make it more likely that he will ask you for help again.

- **Invite him to be your helper.** Offer lots of opportunities to involve him in activities that you are doing, like mixing cake batter, or handing you tools as you put together his new toy. This will allow him to try out his skills without you having to say "no" too much.

Finally, don't be surprised when your independent little man suddenly acts like a helpless baby. Becoming a more capable and separate being can at times feel scary to a toddler. It is quite common for toddlers to revert back to their more infantile ways, at times, in order to be reassured that even though they are now so competent, they will still be taken care of. Don't worry, indulging these needs—like letting him curl up in your arms like a baby, or having you give him a bottle (even if he's been using a cup for months)—won't thwart his development. In fact, it often leads to the toddler giving up the babyish behaviors more quickly.

My 13-month-old has started biting me, and I don't know what to do. He will give me a hug and bite my shoulder or give me a "kiss" and bite my cheek. What's going on? How can I teach him that biting hurts?

The first time that my 14-month-old bit me was at a well-known coffee chain. We had just settled down, she with her milk and me with my latte when bam! She leaned over and "kissed" the fleshy part of my arm. Without thinking, I let out a little shriek of pain—probably scaring the poor barista half to death.

Although not all toddlers do it, biting is a normal behavior for very young children. They do it for any number of reasons: frustration at not being able to express their strong feelings given their limited language skills; feeling threatened when someone invades their space; a desire for attention; or even the seeking of some comfort for sore gums.

Toddlers are also fascinated with cause-and-effect. They are little scientists, testing and researching which behaviors cause which reactions. In fact, they will often perform the same test (biting) with different people to see if they get the same response. This "research" helps very young children understand and organize their world. But it does leave black-and-blues—and sometimes some very hurt feelings.

For young toddlers, like yours, biting behavior is often a temporary phenomenon and fades away as they develop more language ability, grasp the cause–effect connection with biting and realize it's a negative one, or develop enhanced coping skills to help them master their very strong feelings. In your case, it sounds like your son just needs some help expressing his loving and excited feelings in a different way. When he gives you a love-nibble, try to stay calm but stop him in his tracks. Let him know you understand that he is just trying to show you how much he loves you, and demonstrate another way to express himself, such as by kissing you without using his teeth.

In some children, however, biting is more than a brief phase. In either case, it will help to understand when and why your child may be biting, which means being a careful observer. Watching and reading his cues will help you learn more about what stimuli and situations set him up for biting. When and where is he more likely to bite? Is it out of frustration, stress, fear, anger, excitement? Is it when he may be feeling overwhelmed emotionally, or perhaps when he wants some attention? Trying to figure out, as best you can, what is driving the behavior will help you come up with the most sensitive and effective response. So what can parents do?

The natural, immediate reaction to biting—jumping, startling, yelping—are often very effective responses as they let your child know that something is wrong. Next, say in a stern tone with a serious face, "Biting hurts! No biting." Although your child might not understand the actual words now, he soon will. Until then, your expression and tone of voice speak volumes.

As for preventing biting, use what you learned from your observations. If your child tends to bite when overwhelmed, notice when he is showing sign of stress and help him calm down before he "loses it." Validate his feelings: "It feels so bad when someone takes your toy," and give him a firm hug, which often helps children settle down. As he grows, you can help him find other ways to manage his strong feelings, such as putting these feelings into words and offering him alternate ways to work them out—for example, banging a xylophone, stomping his feet, making a lion face and "roaring," doing an angry dance, or drawing his feelings. If he is biting to get attention, help him find other ways to get it. When my son was 2 1/2, much to his chagrin I had the nerve to have another baby. It seemed like every time I sat down to nurse Jessica, he would carry on and sometimes bite me. Having identified this pattern, I started to include him as much as possible—for example, by asking him to pick a book that I could read to him as I nursed. He would flip the pages. Or I would have him sit close to me with some toys and talk with him. The less left out he felt, the less likely he was to act up.

It's important to keep in mind that the bite and the child are separate. Avoid referring to your child as a "biter"—this negative association (in your mind and his) may stick. (In fact, this idea of not labeling your child is a good one to keep in mind in general—for example, not labeling your child as "shy," "bossy," or "whiny".) Also, you will want to partner with your son's child-care provider, if you use one, to decide on a consistent response to biting that both of you feel comfortable using. Finally, bites are bites no matter whom they're from. Whether the bite is minor or serious, be sure to tell your doctor, since the risk of infection is high. Your doctor should immediately examine all bites to the face, hands, or genitals, since these are more likely to involve serious injuries.

Although biting can be a big hot button for parents, remember: *It's not personal.* Think of biting as a form of communication—a message with teeth. If you're consistent in responding to your child's biting, with time you'll find that the only message he's sending with his chompers are smiles.

24 to 36 Months

I Learn About What My Body Can Do

• I can do so much with my fingers and hands: turn the pages of a book, scribble with crayons, and even draw shapes like a circle. I can thread beads with large holes and use kid scissors. I can stir the cake mix, work the VCR and TV remote, and help sort laundry.

• I kick and throw balls. I can stand on one foot. I learn to go up and down the stairs with only one foot on each step!

• I can do so many things for myself—pour milk on my cereal, wash myself in the bathtub, dress myself in simple clothing.

I Learn About My Feelings and Who I Am

• My curiosity can lead me into "off-limits" territory. I need you to keep me safe and to help me learn right from wrong.

• I love my independence, but I also still need you to help me and to do things for me.

• Sometimes I push you away. Other times I want you to hold me close.

• I tune in carefully to your tone and words. I can tell when you are very sad or scared or upset, and sometimes, I feel sad, scared, and upset, too. I know whether you think I am good or bad, pretty or ugly, dumb or smart.

• I am learning self-control. I understand more often what you expect of me. Sometimes I can stop myself from doing things I shouldn't, but not always. I learn to control my behavior when you give me only a few simple, clear rules to follow and help me when I forget.

• I may have new fears—the dark, monsters, people in costumes—because I don't really know the difference between fantasy and reality. My fears can make it hard for me to go to sleep at night and can make me wake up and call out for you.

I Learn About People, Objects, and How Things Work

• I learn how to care for others by the way you care for me. I may rub your back or comfort a friend who is sad.

• I am very tuned in to other kids. I am aware of differences, like gender, age, and skin color.

continued

24 to 36 Months *continued*

- I like to play with other kids. We are getting better at sharing but often will need help.

- I can "play pretend" and use my imagination. I will care for my dolls and animals. I will start to make up stories. I can turn my block tower into a house and even use a block as a phone. When you watch me and join in, you can learn a lot about what I am thinking and feeling. When we play that I'm the mommy going off to work, you see that I am learning to deal with our separations.

- I learn to explore toys and objects in more and more complex ways. I can organize them too—like putting all the toys with wheels together.

I Learn to Communicate and Relate

- I may know up to 200 words in my home language and sometimes in a second language, too.

- I can put words together into sentences.

- I can tell you about things that happened yesterday and about what will happen tomorrow.

- I may get frustrated trying to express myself. I need you to listen patiently. It can help if you put into words what you think I am trying to say because it makes me feel understood and helps me learn new words.

- I also communicate by using my body. I make up dances, songs, and stories, and I draw pictures that tell you what is on my mind.

- I love hearing and reading stories, especially about things I know—like animals, families, and places I have visited.

- Sometimes I like to "read" or tell you a story.

- I like songs, fingerplays (like "Itsy-Bitsy Spider"), and games with nonsense words.

Everywhere I go, I see all these newfangled, electronic toys that say they will make your baby smarter. Is this true? How do I know what kind of toys to get?

Many parents struggle with these questions as they are bombarded by an ever-increasing number of toys that claim to build your baby's brainpower. The bottom line is, there is no short- or long-term research which shows that any of these toys have an impact on brain development. What we do know is that from day one, children are on a mission to learn about the world around them, how it works, and how they can make things happen. The way children do this is largely through play. And the materials we offer them do make a difference. As you make your decisions about what toys or objects to provide for your child, consider the following:

- Babies and toddlers learn through action. The more they have to do to make something happen (i.e., to get their favorite animal to pop up), the more they learn. Toys that do a lot of the "work" for them—those that are more entertaining but require less thinking and problem-solving—will likely be less enriching.

- Young children learn best through experiences that have meaning in their everyday lives. For example, when a 9-month-old learns about object permanence (that things still exist even though he can't see them) by playing hide-and-seek with you, or when you hide rubber ducky under the wash cloth and then make him reappear, your child's learning is more long-lasting because it's part of his everyday life, and mostly because he is making his discovery in partnership with you! So think of yourself as your child's most important and favorite toy, and make everyday moments like bathing, diapering, or taking a walk an opportunity to promote your child's learning. Interacting with you beats a battery-operated stuffed bear any day.

- Everyday objects, especially those that mimic what children see in their world, are often most interesting to young children— and they are great tools for learning. This is because young children love to imitate, which is a good thing because it is how they learn new skills and feel competent. It is also a way for them to feel close to you. The great news about these everyday objects is that they are either free (because they are safe objects you already have, such as wooden spoons, plastic containers, or old clothing) or at least much less costly than high-tech toys.

- Helping to build a young child's imagination is one of the most important ways that parents foster both emotional and cognitive intelligence. It is through pretend play that children develop higher-level thinking skills that are important for math, science, and creative and abstract thinking. Pretend play also helps them work through many important issues such as separation (i.e., pretending that they are the moms who are leaving for work) or sibling rivalry (acting out their anger on the "pretend" baby rather than the real one!). One concern about some of these high-tech toys is that they often focus on rote skills, such as memorizing numbers, and not on developing imagination. Further, many of these toys, such as the dolls or animals that "talk" and have their own personalities, limit children's use of their own imaginations because they can't project their own thoughts and feelings onto these toys to create their own "stories."

So, before you buy a new toy for your child, ask yourself . . .What will my child learn from this object? What will he have to do to make it work? For example, will it help him learn to use his fingers to manipulate objects? Will he have to problem-solve? Will it encourage him to use his imagination? Can he use it in a variety of ways or will he tire of it quickly? Asking yourself these questions will help you make good decisions.

My 2-year-old always has to have her way—from what she wears to the bowl she uses for cereal. How can I get her to be more flexible?

A flexible toddler—is it possible? Actually, what looks and feels like total inflexibility is a natural and important part of your child's growth, and signals a leap in her development. Two-year-olds are at a stage when their sense of self is emerging. They are strong-willed, they know what they want and don't want, and they have the communication skills to tell you just how they feel.

At the same time, children this age are more involved in the world around them. They have a lot more to manage each day as they take in new experiences and encounter new people. Their world becomes less predictable. To feel secure, they desperately seek to control whatever they can. This need for sameness and predictability makes routines especially important. As trivial as it may seem, using the same bowl may be an important part of your child's daily ritual and help her feel "okay."

It is also in the toddler years that the concept of ownership is beginning to take root. This new understanding of "mine" is important to your child's growing sense of self. You can see how their sense of ownership and need for predictability can lead toddlers to assert more control over their world.

Furthermore, temperament plays a big role in a child's flexibility. Children who are more cautious and slow-to-warm up need more consistency to feel safe, and thus may seem less flexible than their more easygoing peers. The challenge for parents is how to respect their child's unique needs while helping her learn how to adapt when things don't go her way. An important part of how you do this is by setting sensible limits. Whether it's about choosing what to wear or what dish to use, accepting limits—that she can't always get what she wants—is an essential part of a child's development as it will help her function successfully in the real world with all of its rules and expectations.

So when your child is demanding something that you don't feel is appropriate, see it as an opportunity—a teachable moment. You can use the following six steps to help her become more flexible while respecting her temperament, acknowledging her feelings and needs, and offering her real choices.

1. **Decide if the behavior needs to be modified**, also known as "choosing your battles." Get clear on why you don't like the behavior, and balance that against what you think your child needs. For example, can you allow your toddler to wear mismatching socks when you are someone who values coordinated clothing?

   Also, consider the circumstances. If she is in a more vulnerable place, perhaps due to illness or a major change such as a move or a long separation from you—or she's simply having a bad morning—you may decide to clean the bowl and give it to her.

   If you do decide to set the limit, proceed with the following steps:

2. **Validate your child's feelings:** "I know you really want the blue bowl. It's your special bowl, and you don't like using other bowls." (If you skip this step, your child is likely to "up the ante" and show you just how much she wants that blue bowl . . . often, this is when tantrums start.)

3. **Set the limit:** "But the blue bowl is dirty, so we can't use it right now."

4. **Offer limited choices,** all of which must be acceptable to you. "You can use the red bowl or the yellow bowl. Which would you like?"

5. **Help her cope with her disappointment by problem-solving:** "Tomorrow morning, when the dishwasher is done, you can use the blue bowl for your cereal." If your child doesn't accept the choices you've offered or has a tantrum, *remain calm and reinforce your expectation:* "Okay, it doesn't look like you want either bowl. I'll leave them here on the counter. If you change your mind and want to use one for your ice cream, let me know."

6. **Don't give in once you have set the limit.** She will just learn that if she pushes hard enough, she'll get what she wants. This will also make it harder the next time you try to enforce a limit.

The two's are a challenging time because children are growing and changing so rapidly. This is what also makes them so interesting and fun. Up until now, most parents have enjoyed a feeling of control over their child's day-to-day life. Now, your daughter is dead-set on controlling her world… and so are you. Both of you need to adapt to this new relationship. (And it's good practice for when she becomes a teen!)

Both my husband and I are very outgoing, social people, but our 2-year-old is terribly shy. He won't leave my side at the park or at birthday parties, and he also doesn't have many friends at preschool. How did we get such a timid child? And what can we do to get him to be more outgoing?

It can be quite challenging to have a child whose personality and way of approaching the world are very different from yours. The good news is that you've taken the first and most important step. You have acknowledged the difference, which means that you are a good observer of your child and that you are self-aware. This understanding will enable you to sensitively nurture your child's development. This may or may not lead to his becoming more outgoing, but it will help him manage his feelings and adapt more easily to social environments.

The way you are describing your son has to do with what we call temperament—a person's individual way of approaching the world. It's something we are born with—*not something parents create*. What *is* our responsibility as parents is to understand who our child is and to respect and accept his individual needs, not to try to make him into someone we want him to be.

Your careful and sensitive observation of your son has given you very valuable information about how to best parent him. His behavior is telling you that new situations, and especially those that involve lots of people and activity, feel overwhelming and uncomfortable. This is why he hangs back, doesn't jump right into the action, and looks for support from you. He is "slow-to-warm-up." He needs time to observe and become more familiar with his surroundings in order to feel less anxious and in control of the situation before he is able to join in.

It also sounds like your son may be a child who is more comfortable in one-on-one interaction than in large groups. He may indeed prefer to have one or two close friends rather than a whole bunch. What's important to remember is that there is not one way for a child to be happy; what feels good to one person may not feel good to another. It sounds like for you and your husband, having lots of friends and trying new things may be what brings you pleasure and fulfillment. What makes your son feel content and good about himself may be quite different. Again, what's important is your ability to separate your needs from his, and to respond sensitively to his cues. What will make him happy is your respect for and acceptance of his individual needs, which will let him know that he is liked, valued, and loved. This will help him form healthy relationships and give him the confidence to try new things as he grows.

At the same time that you are validating and respecting his needs and feelings, there is a lot that you can do to help your son adapt and enjoy social relationships:

- Prepare him for a new situation. For example, if he is going to a birthday party, talk with him about it in advance. As he gets older, let him know that you understand that parties can feel hard for him. Make a plan together for how he can manage his feelings—perhaps arriving a few minutes early to feel comfortable before all the other kids arrive, or going to the party with a friend whom he feels safe with so that he has a "partner."

- When he clings to you for support, acknowledge his need to stay close to you. Let him sit on your lap, and talk about what you see happening around you. Then suggest that you explore together. Check out the games that they are playing, see if he will take a turn with you by his side. Or you can take a turn first. If you are at the park, go down the slide together, sit by his side at the sandbox, watch and talk about what the other kids are doing.

- Provide lots of opportunities for your son to interact with others. Find out from his teachers who your son does interact with, or ask them to identify a child whom they feel would be compatible with him. Invite that child over for some playdates. This will give your child a chance to interact with peers in a less demanding environment and affords the opportunity for you to provide support to your son—for example, by getting a game going among the three of you.

The key is to join your child where he is at, provide the support he needs to feel safe and comfortable, and then help him adapt.

How do I wean my baby (20 months) off her pacifier? We've been using it since she was born. She goes to sleep with it and uses it to calm herself down when she's upset.

I hate to answer a question with a question, but why do you want to wean your child from the pacifier? If it is interfering in her functioning—such as interacting, talking, or playing with others—then it may be a good idea. But if she is using it only to get herself to sleep (better than relying on you to rock her, feed her, or lie down with her) and to soothe herself when upset, she is using it to a good end. Learning to soothe oneself is a very important skill that we all need to develop.

Although many parents are concerned about the impact of using the pacifier on their child's teeth, at her age this is not a cause for concern. Pediatric orthodontists report that regular use of a pacifier before age 3 to 4 is nothing to worry about and does not cause dental problems or misaligned teeth. Also important to keep in mind is that children who are dependent on their pacifiers often just substitute with their thumbs if the pacifier is taken away. Finally, getting into a power struggle over the pacifier is what may be most harmful. Your child may hold onto it more fiercely. And until she has developed other ways to soothe herself, she may have a hard time calming herself down. Rest assured, even the children who fiercely hold onto the pacifier almost always give it up on their own once they are in a child-care or preschool setting where other children are not using pacifiers.

Having said that, if you still want to wean your child from the pacifier, here are some things to think about and try:

- Because it seems that your child is using the pacifier as a way to self-soothe, it will be important to help her find other ways to calm herself before you actually take it away. A "lovey" can help. Many children use them for comfort. If she doesn't have a lovey, you can help her develop one by choosing a favorite blanket, stuffed animal, or doll and including that object in your caretaking activities. Have it sit on her or your lap as you read, sit next to her as she eats, sing and cuddle with you during the bedtime routine.

- Do it gradually. Taking the pacifier away at bedtime will probably be the most difficult, so you may not want to start then. When she wants the pacifier during the day, let her have it for a minute or two and then offer other ways to help her calm down—a hug from you, reading a book together. Reduce the time you let her have it until she doesn't use it at all. Do something similar at bedtime. Perhaps let her have it during book reading and rocking or singing but not when she goes down to sleep.

- Have a pacifier going-away party. Rituals can help with transitions. Together, gather up all her pacifiers, put them in a special place (like a box that she can help decorate), sing some good-bye songs, and then put the box away.

Keep in mind as you consider how to proceed that an incremental and sensitive approach will make it much more likely that your plan will succeed.

My 2½-year-old's daycare teacher has been telling me that my son hits and is very aggressive with the other kids. He's not talking yet, so it's hard for me to know what is going on with him and to discipline him. What can I do?

First of all, aggressive behavior in toddlers is not uncommon. They have strong feelings that they express in many different ways, often through action. Aggression can be the result of many different things—frustration that they can't do or have everything they want, difficulty managing strong emotions, recent changes in their lives (new baby, parent on a business trip), and countless other reasons. Key to effectively addressing the behavior is understanding why your child is feeling angry and "acting out" at this time.

One hypothesis, based on your description of your child, is that his behavior is connected to his language development. By age 2½, most children have a growing vocabulary and can string several words together, such as, "I want truck!" to communicate what they are thinking and feeling. Sometimes children this age don't have the words but are able to communicate through gestures (such as pointing) and vocalizations or through single words (such as, "Mine!"), which let others know what they want.

Children who are unable to communicate well often use actions to express themselves, like hitting the child who has the truck he wants. In addition, when a child is unable to let others know what he needs, that in itself can be frustrating and can lead to aggressive behavior.

Given your child's difficulty in using words, the first step I would suggest is getting a language assessment by a speech therapist. A speech therapist can help you understand your child's language development, which will help determine whether his behavior is tied to a developmental issue like a delay in learning language or to another issue. You can get referrals to a speech therapist from your child's health care provider or from a local child development center. These assessments are not invasive. Typically, a speech therapist will assess a child through play and other activities. You should be an important part of the assessment—sharing your observations of and ideas about your child (indeed, you know him best)—and be present in the actual session(s). These assessments can be very useful in identifying if and where your son's challenges lie and in developing a plan to help him learn good communication skills that will hopefully lead to "using his words" and learning other ways to express his anger in nonaggressive ways.